Light of the World

Family Devotional

90 Devotions for Families Who Want to Be Like Jesus

TYNDALE KIDS

Salvation Poem™ PROJECT

I0793656

Visit Tyndale's website for kids at tyndale.com/kids.

Learn more about Salvation Poem Project at salvationpoem.com.
Learn more about *Light of the World* at lightoftheworld.com.

Tyndale is a registered trademark of Tyndale House Ministries. The Tyndale Kids logo is a trademark of Tyndale House Ministries.

Light of the World Family Devotional: 90 Devotions for Families Who Want to Be Like Jesus

Copyright © 2025 by The Salvation Poem Foundation, Inc. All rights reserved.

Cover illustration copyright © 2025 by The Salvation Poem Foundation, Inc. All rights reserved.

Author photograph copyright © 2023 by Natalie Hanemann. All rights reserved.

Illustrations copyright © 2025 by The Salvation Poem Foundation, Inc. All rights reserved.

Cover design by Jacqueline L. Nuñez

Cover illustration by Tony Bancroft and Darnell Johnson

Interior design by Josh Meyer and Darnell Johnson

Published in association with Mary DeMuth Literary, MaryDeMuthLiterary.com.

Scripture quotations are taken from the *Holy Bible*, New Living Translation, copyright © 1996, 2004, 2015 by Tyndale House Foundation. Used by permission of Tyndale House Publishers, Carol Stream, Illinois 60188. All rights reserved.

The URLs in this book were verified prior to publication. The publisher is not responsible for content in the links, links that have expired, or websites that have changed ownership after that time.

For manufacturing information regarding this product, please call 1-855-277-9400.

For information about special discounts for bulk purchases, please contact Tyndale House Publishers at csresponse@tyndale.com, or call 1-855-277-9400.

ISBN 979-8-4005-1510-1

Printed in the United States of America

31 30 29 28 27 26 25

7 6 5 4 3 2 1

1 Made in God's Image

So God created human beings in his own image. In the image of God he created them; male and female he created them.

GENESIS 1:27

As the film begins, little John and James ask their mother Salome to tell them the creation story. Over lamplight, she gathers them close and tells the story they had heard many times in the synagogue. She says, "In the beginning was nothing but darkness. Then God said, let there be *light*! Over six days, he spoke all things into existence, and then he made us in his image. His children, created in his image. We lived with him together in a perfect garden. There was just one rule: Do not eat from the forbidden tree. But we didn't trust him. We disobeyed, and in our shame, we fled from God's light, into a dark and dying world. Our world."

Questions for Discussion

Isn't it awesome to think that God created the entire world—all the animals, plants, rivers, and stars—simply by speaking? That's one powerful God! What's even more amazing is that God decided that we would be his most important creation.

What do you think it means to be made in God's image? Does it mean that we are supposed to create things, like he does? Or maybe that we were supposed to share his attributes of love, mercy, and compassion?

It likely means many things. However, the most important part is that he made us to be his children, living in a loving, obedient relationship with him. But humans broke that loving, obedient relationship when we sinned. This is why we experience death, because we gave up our purpose and embraced sin instead of God.

What do you think it would be like to live in the garden of Eden with God?

Where everything was perfect, and there was no sin, and people lived forever?

Prayer

Lord, bring us back to living in perfect relationship with you! We want to obey you and to make you proud of us, Father, but we can't obey unless you first change us. So, change us to be like you and give us the strength to do good and to say no to evil. Amen.

Bible Verse

For God made Christ, who never sinned, to be the offering for our sin, so that we could be made right with God through Christ.
2 CORINTHIANS 5:21

2 God Will Save Us

But I will call on God, and the LORD will rescue me.
PSALM 55:16

As John and James' mother Salome recounts the story of how the first people fell into sin and darkness, John interrupts, crying, "Wait, mama! I don't like the dark. We're scared . . . right, James?"

James says, "Yeah, maybe just skip to the part where *You-Know-Who* shows up?"

Salome continues, "Don't worry, I was just getting to the best part! Separated from God's light, what hope did we have, alone in the darkness? But God did not abandon us. He promised to send a mighty king to save us. The Messiah! He will overcome the darkness and make everything right again."

James jumps in and says, "Yeah, by destroying our enemies! His Kingdom of Light will last forever!"

And John says, "He'll defeat Rome and free us all!"

Questions for Discussion

We all have troubles that we wish God would take away. Maybe we don't want to go to school, or maybe someone we love is sick. What's the one biggest thing that, given the chance, you would ask God to fix right now? Take turns sharing as a family and then write down your requests and pray about them.

God tells us to take all our requests to him, but sometimes we don't want what God wants. John and James are tired of seeing the Romans hurt people they love, and they want God to do something about it. After all, God is a righteous judge. That means he wants to fix it all! Right?

When they finally meet the Messiah, however, he's nothing like what they imagined. He isn't this big, strong warrior who cuts down the Romans with a flaming sword. In fact, he heals Romans and preaches God's good news to them! In the end, Jesus even lets himself be killed. It is the opposite of what they thought would save them. Yet it is exactly what they needed. In fact, it's also the only thing that could truly change the hearts and behavior of the Romans.

Sometimes, when God saves us, it's not in the ways we expected. Be sure to keep track of the prayers you prayed today and write down how God answers them.

Prayer

God, we know you hear all our requests, and we are thankful that you care about each and every one of them. Give us wisdom to see your will and give us hearts that want what you want! Amen.

Bible Verse

But everyone who calls on the name of the LORD will be saved.
ACTS 2:21

3 Focus on What's Real

He said to Thomas, "Put your finger here, and look at my hands. Put your hand into the wound in my side. Don't be faithless any longer. Believe!" "My Lord and my God!" Thomas exclaimed. Then Jesus told him, "You believe because you have seen me. Blessed are those who believe without seeing me."
JOHN 20:27-29

At the start of the film, we hear John's father Zebedee say to his wife Salome, "We have to focus on what's real."

Some people struggle to believe God is real because we can't see him. God the Father doesn't have a body—he is spirit. Same with the Holy Spirit. But God the Son, Jesus, became flesh "and made his home among us" (John 1:14). This is called the incarnation, which literally means "to take on flesh." Often when we think of God, we imagine Jesus because it is much easier to imagine a person than a spirit.

Questions for Discussion

How do we know something is real if we can't see it and touch it?

Let's do some role-playing as a family. Team one only believes a thing is real if we can use our five senses to prove it. Team two believes things can exist that can't be seen, touched, smelled, heard, or tasted.

Now, debate the following topic: Does love exist or not?

Prayer

Jesus, sometimes I wish I could have lived when you were on earth so I could have talked to you myself. I'm here two thousand years later and have to rely on stories written by people who witnessed your life. When I pray, I want to imagine speaking to you directly, but I also sometimes like to imagine praying to God the Father or the Holy Spirit. Because they don't have any physical features, I use my imagination. I don't need to see you to know you're real. Thank you for the gift of faith. Amen.

Bible Verse

For God is Spirit, so those who worship him must worship in spirit and in truth.

JOHN 4:24

4 Do Something!

Do not withhold good from those who deserve it when it's in your power to help them.
PROVERBS 3:27

Have you ever seen something bad happening to a friend or neighbor, but you were too afraid to say something? Or maybe you thought that you couldn't say anything because you're just a kid. In the movie, John's family overhears a commotion in the street. They rush out to see a Roman soldier dragging off Peter and Andrew's dad because he couldn't pay his taxes.

It's upsetting to see someone being dragged away from their home and family! At the time, Roman soldiers collected more taxes than most Jewish families could afford. Rome took more money than was fair, and this caused the Jews to feel angry.

John and James want to rush outside and help, but their papa stops them. "We have to keep our heads down and take care of ourselves." This makes the family feel even worse because they are helpless. John responds, with tears in his eyes, "They need our help!" When the kids go to bed, Zebedee goes across the road and helps Peter's family.

Questions for Discussion

Share a time when you saw someone in trouble and wanted to help. (Parents, share first.)

Have you ever seen someone in need, but inside, you really didn't want to take the time or energy to help them? Maybe when your mom comes home from the grocery store and asks you to help her unload the car? Or when you finish an assignment at school and the teacher asks you to help a classmate who is struggling?

It can be hard to be kind to our neighbor or friend. If Jesus had been with John and James's family and saw the Romans taking their friend's dad away, do you think he would have told them to keep their heads down and take care of themselves?

Someone a long time ago said that the only thing necessary for evil to triumph is for good people to do nothing. What can we do next time we see someone who is being unfairly treated or who needs our help? You see, Jesus never tires of helping those who need it, because he loves them. The more we act like Jesus on the outside and do things he would do, the more we become like him on the inside and the more our hearts fill up with love.

Prayer

Jesus, please give me the courage to stand up for someone who needs my help. I may not know exactly what to say or do, but I trust you to use me for your greater purpose. Amen.

Bible Verse

I am giving you a new commandment: Love each other. Just as I have loved you, you should love each other. Your love for one another will prove to the world that you are my disciples.

JOHN 13:34-35

5 Never Too Late for Faith

God saved you by his grace when you believed.
And you can't take credit for this; it is a gift from God.
EPHESIANS 2:8

John's papa Zebedee thinks the Messiah is just a story. But the fishmonger tells John that the Messiah is real! What do you think the difference is between one person who believes and another who thinks it's make-believe?

Zebedee doesn't yet have faith. Our faith in Jesus' salvation is a gift. But like any gift, before we can enjoy it, we have to receive it. Jesus offers the gift to everyone, but not everyone chooses to accept it. The good news is that we have the chance to accept Jesus' gift of faith until we take our very last breath! It's never too late to have faith.

Questions for Discussion

What are some ways you've let Jesus know that you accept his gift of faith?

Have you ever met someone—maybe at school or in your neighborhood—who doesn't believe in Jesus? Were you shy to share what you believe? Have you ever spoken to a friend about Jesus?

Let's role-play as a family and imagine how it might look to talk to a friend about who Jesus is and what he's done for us. (Take turns so both the parent and child get to represent the one with faith and the one without faith.)

Prayer

Lord, thank you for offering me the gift of faith. Without you, I would be nothing. Give me the words to tell others about you so they can receive the gift of your salvation. Amen.

Bible Verse

Faith shows the reality of what we hope for; it is the evidence of things we cannot see.
HEBREWS 11:1

6 You Will Have Trouble

We can rejoice, too, when we run into problems and trials, for we know that they help us develop endurance. And endurance develops strength of character, and character strengthens our confident hope of salvation. And this hope will not lead to disappointment. For we know how dearly God loves us, because he has given us the Holy Spirit to fill our hearts with his love.

ROMANS 5:3-5

John is trusted to take the bag of fish into town to sell to the fishmonger. The money John gets will pay for the taxes his family owes Rome. Tension is high because the tax collector Matthew is on his way to their house to get the money. If they can't pay the exact amount owed, they'll have to pay extra. John's dad Zebedee may even be dragged off to jail, like their neighbor's dad was the other night. But John runs into trouble at the market, and by the time he gets home, he only has one coin to show for the sale.

Questions for Discussion

Have you ever been trusted to do something important, but along the way, you ran into problems? Maybe you forgot your school assignment at home, so the teacher took off points for it being late. Or maybe you were asked not to touch anything, but you accidentally knocked over something valuable. Can you describe how it may have felt when this happened? (Parents, share first.)

Jesus ran into a lot of problems with the big responsibility entrusted to him by the Father. People were angry with him, accused him of crimes he didn't commit, and even tried to stone him. But God protected Jesus, and he protects us too. Bad things may still happen—in fact, Jesus tells us we can count on it, but he also reminds us not to worry. Bad times will pass, and in the end, we can trust that all will be well. The battle between good and evil has already been fought. And we won.

Prayer

God, some days are hard, but I trust that you are with me. Help me to be responsible when trusted to do an important task and keep me safe when trouble comes. Thank you for all the ways you love me. I want you to know I love you too! Amen.

Bible Verse

I have told you all this so that you may have peace in me. Here on earth you will have many trials and sorrows. But take heart, because I have overcome the world.

JOHN 16:33

7 Notice When Someone Is Suffering

Let everyone see that you are considerate in all you do. Remember, the Lord is coming soon. Don't worry about anything; instead, pray about everything. Tell God what you need, and thank him for all he has done. Then you will experience God's peace, which exceeds anything we can understand. His peace will guard your hearts and minds as you live in Christ Jesus.

PHILIPPIANS 4:5-7

On the way back from the fishmonger's stall, a carpenter points out to John a shortcut to get home. (Any guesses as to who that may have been?) As John is walking down the alley, he feels nervous and a bit scared by what he sees. A mom holding a crying child, a man sleeping on the ground, even a woman who appears to be possessed by a bad spirit. As he's leaving the shadowed area, he hears a child cough. He turns back and notices a young boy sitting against the wall, flushed with fever. John takes one of the coins in his hand and gives it to the boy, whose face lights up.

Questions for Discussion

We can fail to notice when people around us are suffering. Sometimes even when we notice it, it can make us uncomfortable because we aren't sure what to do. Think for a moment and share the last person you saw who was in pain, was sick, or seemed very sad. (Take turns sharing.)

Jesus paid special attention to people who were suffering. Though it is hard to think about, we also know that Jesus suffered when he died on the cross.

What is one way you can show God's love to someone who is in pain? Would you be comfortable going up to speak with them? Offering them one of your snacks or last week's allowance money? Most importantly, we can pray for them to be made well and to know how much the Lord loves them.

Prayer

Make me more aware, Lord, of the people around me who are suffering so I can show them your love and compassion. Help me to see you in the eyes of the poor, the stranger, and the sick. Amen.

Bible Verse

God blesses those who patiently endure testing and temptation. Afterward they will receive the crown of life that God has promised to those who love him.
JAMES 1:12

8 Those You Help May One Day Help You

Suppose you see a brother or sister who has no food or clothing, and you say, "Good-bye and have a good day; stay warm and eat well"—but then you don't give that person any food or clothing. What good does that do?

JAMES 2:15-16

John gives little Josiah a coin because he feels compassion for the boy, who clearly doesn't have much and is sick. A few minutes later, the Roman guard Lucius spots John and comes after him. Unbeknownst to Lucius, Josiah has tied the Roman's red cloak to a wagon. Thanks to Josiah's quick thinking, John is able to get away and make it home to his father, who is waiting for the money to pay the tax collector.

There's only one problem: John's escape only makes Lucius even angrier, because now he's been made to look like a fool in public.

Questions for Discussion

I bet John never expected that he'd get help from little Josiah, and yet John's act of kindness inspires Josiah to help when he sees the opportunity. It won't always happen, but our kindness is sometimes repaid in surprising ways. It's not the reason we help, but it sure is a bonus!

Can you remember a time when you chose to help someone in need? Tell your family about it.

Prayer

Jesus, you helped so many people in need when you were here. Give me eyesight that makes me more aware of those around me who are in need. Even I can make a small difference in the world, thanks to you. Amen.

Bible Verse

If you help the poor, you are lending to the Lord—and he will repay you!

PROVERBS 19:17

The LORD is slow to anger and filled with unfailing love, forgiving every kind of sin and rebellion.
NUMBERS 14:18

When John returns home without more than a single coin for the fish he sold, Matthew is already at their house, waiting to be paid. Zebedee is unable to pay the taxes, and Matthew offers them a three-day extension, but what they owe will go up. They already owe so much, so this "deal" adds to their burden. John gets so angry, he loses his temper and yells at Matthew, "You're a traitor to your own people. One day you're gonna get yours!" You see, Matthew is a Jew who works for Rome, collecting money from the Jewish people. Many Jews saw this as a betrayal. But John's anger has a severe consequence he didn't intend: Matthew doubles the amount Zebedee owes.

Questions for Discussion

Everyone gets angry. It's our natural response when something unfair happens. What do you think about the way John handled himself? (Take turns sharing.)

Can you think of a time when you got angry and lost your temper? How did you feel when it was happening? How did you feel afterward?

The Bible tells us the Lord is slow to anger and quick to forgive. That's a good thing because we never want our actions to anger God!

Prayer

Lord, it is hard to keep calm when something unfair happens. I want to be slow to anger, like you. Be with me when my anger gets too big and stay with me until I can calm down. I can't do that without your help, Jesus. Thank you for helping me become a better person. Amen.

Bible Verse

And "don't sin by letting anger control you." Don't let the sun go down while you are still angry, for anger gives a foothold to the devil.

EPHESIANS 4:26-27

Do not twist justice in legal matters by favoring the poor or being partial to the rich and powerful. Always judge people fairly.
LEVITICUS 19:15

When Matthew offers to "help" by extending the due date on the tax money by three days, he also increases the amount John's family owes. When John hears this, he erupts in anger and shouts, "That's not fair!"

He's right; it's not fair. Yet, that was one way Rome took advantage of the Jewish people. They weren't good rulers. The Roman occupiers didn't understand Jewish religion or practices, and they treated the Jews like dogs. Rome was much more powerful than Israel, so unfortunately, there was little the Jews could do to break free from them.

Questions for Discussion

Have you ever thought, *That's not fair!* when someone in authority punished you? Have everyone share a time when this happened.

It can feel so frustrating to not be able to defend yourself to those in charge. How do you handle those feelings?

A few healthy ways to blow off steam might be to run outside, listen to music, or journal your feelings. The important part is to not bottle up all your big emotions, or else they'll come out in other, less healthy ways.

Prayer

God, when people aren't fair, it really upsets me. But your Word teaches that one day all the unfairness will be made right because you see everything and will settle the score. This gives me comfort and calms me down. I'm grateful that you will make all things fair one day. Amen.

Bible Verse

I said to myself, "In due season God will judge everyone, both good and bad, for all their deeds."
ECCLESIASTES 3:17

There is no greater love than to lay down one's life for one's friends.
JOHN 15:13

James can't help his dad catch fish because he injured his elbow when John lost his temper. Peter comes to help and tells Zebedee, "Listen, when they came for my father, you were the only one who took care of my family. All these years, you showed up. Now it's my turn to show up." So even though Peter has his own fish to catch, he sacrifices to help Zebedee's family in a time of great need.

Questions for Discussion

When we love someone, there are times when we must sacrifice for them even though it means we lose something as a result. Peter's family owes taxes too, but instead of fishing for money to pay those taxes, he offers to help Zebedee and his family. What's the cost of him doing this?

Love means wanting goodness for someone else, even if it costs you something. We sacrifice something of value for the good of someone else when we tithe at church or give money to someone experiencing homelessness.

Can you think of something you could do at home to show your love for a family member? Something you may not particularly want to do, but by doing it, you are lightening the load of your siblings or your mom and dad?

Parents, can you think of one thing you could do for each of your children to make their day a little easier?

Once you've done this, share how it felt to sacrifice for someone you love.

Prayer

Lord, you sacrificed your life so that we may have the chance to be in heaven with you. All you require from us is faith in your salvation. I want others to accept this gift. Please increase the love in my heart so I can make the world a little bit better. Thank you for your sacrifice! Amen.

Bible Verse

For this is how God loved the world: He gave his one and only Son, so that everyone who believes in him will not perish but have eternal life.

JOHN 3:16

One day as Jesus was walking along the shore of the Sea of Galilee, he saw two brothers—Simon, also called Peter, and Andrew—throwing a net into the water, for they fished for a living. Jesus called out to them, "Come, follow me, and I will show you how to fish for people!" And they left their nets at once and followed him.

MATTHEW 4:18-20

John feels like nothing he does helps anyone, and this makes him sad. When he goes to sit with his mom, who is mending fishing nets, she sees his frustration. She puts her arm around him and tells him she sees the fishing nets like a promise from God. The fisherman's job isn't to catch the fish; it's to cast the net. Then he sits and waits . . . and trusts God to provide the fish.

She says, "Even when we find ourselves adrift in the deepest, darkest waters, even when all hope is lost . . . we still cast our nets and trust they won't come up empty."

Questions for Discussion

John's mom sees that he is upset, and she explains the importance of trusting God. Why do you think she talked to him about trust?

Have you ever heard the saying "If it is to be, it's up to me"? There's just one problem with this idea. We aren't nearly as strong as we think we are. That's a hard idea to accept, especially when we hear from coaches and teachers (and even parents!) to push harder, do more, give it all we've got. These encouragements aren't bad—they just leave out the most powerful source we have when trying to accomplish anything . . . God. Like David, who found the courage to go to battle with a giant, when we trust God to be our strength, he shows up every time.

The next time you're facing an obstacle that takes all your strength, remind yourself, "Pray first!"

Prayer

Send down your Spirit, Jesus, in those times when all hope feels lost so that I remember that you are my source of strength. I can always count on you. Amen.

Bible Verse

Do not be afraid or discouraged, for the LORD will personally go ahead of you. He will be with you; he will neither fail you nor abandon you."

DEUTERONOMY 31:8

A little farther up the shore Jesus saw Zebedee's sons, James and John, in a boat repairing their nets. He called them at once, and they also followed him, leaving their father, Zebedee, in the boat with the hired men.
MARK 1:19-20

Did you realize that within the twelve apostles there were two sets of brothers? James and John, and Peter and Andrew. Sibling relationships can be complicated—one minute you're best friends, the next you're fighting and calling each other names.

A lot of the tension between siblings has to do with comparison. In the film, when John goes to the fishmonger, even he starts comparing John to his brother James. He says, "Your father normally sends the other bigger one—you know, the stronger one, the one that seems a little smarter . . . the more handsome one."

Later, when John wants to help catch fish, James says, "I don't think my brother is cut out to be a fisherman," referencing John's clumsiness.

Questions for Discussion

Imagine Jesus asks you *and* your sibling to follow him. Do you think that might cause some tension? Even though it is natural to compare yourself to your sibling, comparison never leads anywhere good. Fortunately, God doesn't have favorites, and he doesn't compare us to each other. He loves us all the same, even though we are all so different.

Ask your parents if they ever fought with their siblings growing up.

Learning to get along with people who think differently than you is part of growing up. The next time you and your sibling (or if you are an only child, your friend) have an argument, try to remember that we are all made in God's image and deserve to be treated with dignity. Peace begins with us.

Prayer

I can get so annoyed at my sibling(s), Lord. Before I resort to hurtful words or take physical action, make me mindful that though we fight, I love them. Loving people that we disagree with is so hard! But you show us how it's done. Thank you for my family, God. Amen.

Bible Verse

Andrew, Simon Peter's brother, was one of these men who heard what John said and then followed Jesus. Andrew went to find his brother, Simon, and told him, "We have found the Messiah" (which means "Christ"). Then Andrew brought Simon to meet Jesus. Looking intently at Simon, Jesus said, "Your name is Simon, son of John—but you will be called Cephas" (which means "Peter").

JOHN 1:40-42

I tell you the truth, of all who have ever lived, none is greater than John the Baptist. Yet even the least person in the Kingdom of Heaven is greater than he is!
MATTHEW 11:11

John the Baptist is often depicted as a quirky and offbeat character, probably because he lived in the desert and ate honey and locusts (mmm, sweet and crunchy!). John the Baptist tells little John that we get baptized to start over because we've all done things we shouldn't have. He says, "Baptism is a way of saying to God, 'I turn away from my darkness, and I choose your light instead.'"

Even Jesus got baptized by John the Baptist. When Jesus rose from the water, the heavens split open and a voice said, "This is my dearly loved Son, who brings me great joy" (Matthew 3:17). Jesus' baptism marked the beginning of his three-year public ministry. When he left the waters of baptism, he headed into the dry desert to face temptation.

Questions for Discussion

If you've been baptized, do you remember your own baptism? If you were too young, ask your parents to tell you about the day you were baptized. Was it done in a church or outside? Was water sprinkled on your head or were you fully dunked underwater? Did you celebrate afterward?

Think of how refreshing it is when you go to the pool in the summertime and you first go underwater. If it's a hot day, the water feels cold and a bit jarring at first. Nothing quite compares to that feeling. Water not only literally washes away the dirt on our skin, but in baptism, water symbolically washes away our sins. We are made new again.

Prayer

Jesus, I hope we always stay close. No matter what I've done, you forgive me when I am sorry in my heart. I don't have to earn your love because you give it to me freely. I can never express how thankful I am to be yours. Amen.

Bible Verse

Then I will sprinkle clean water on you, and you will be clean. Your filth will be washed away, and you will no longer worship idols. And I will give you a new heart, and I will put a new spirit in you. I will take out your stony, stubborn heart and give you a tender, responsive heart. And I will put my Spirit in you so that you will follow my decrees and be careful to obey my regulations.

EZEKIEL 36:25-27

And the one sitting on the throne said, "Look, I am making everything new!" And then he said to me, "Write this down, for what I tell you is trustworthy and true."
REVELATION 21:5

When the Baptizer is talking with John, he says, "There's nothing so broken that God can't fix it."

We make mistakes, and our actions can cause us to feel guilt, sadness, or anger. When we carry these emotions around, they build up and become more intense. It's best to express ourselves in healthy ways—not by throwing a tantrum or losing our temper, but by talking about our feelings, drawing, or doing something active.

We all need a fresh start at some point. No one does everything perfectly all the time. That's impossible. God loves us so much that he wants to shower us with love and forgiveness. And that's not something we have to earn. He gives it freely.

Questions for Discussion

Have you ever wished you had a time machine so you could go back and make better choices? This is something everyone wishes for, at least once in their lives.

Let's have a little fun. If you could pick a time in the past to visit, what time would you choose and why? Have everyone share their answers. If you could go back in time to one event from Jesus' life, which event would you pick?

Prayer

I don't ever want to do bad things, God, but if I do, I feel so lucky that your forgiveness comes when I say just two little words: I'm sorry. Please help me remember to apologize to those I've hurt and remind me that when others apologize to me, forgiving them makes me more like you. Amen.

Bible Verse

He heals the brokenhearted and bandages their wounds.

PSALM 147:3

**And you must love the LORD your God with all your heart,
all your soul, and all your strength.
DEUTERONOMY 6:5**

The Pharisees do not like what John the Baptist is doing. They feel threatened by his approach to worshiping God through repentance. They believe the best way to get close to God is by strictly practicing the laws God gave through Moses. Some of those laws included ritual cleansings and offering the blood of lambs for atonement. The law is not bad, but when we obsess over who is or isn't keeping the law, we can lose sight of something more important: love. God also told Moses that we are to love one another as we love ourselves. The best combination is to obey the law AND love others at the same time. But at times, that can be really hard.

Questions for Discussion

It's natural to want clear boundaries—our God is a God of order. Laws make us feel safe and keep us from misbehaving in a way that could hurt others. Imagine if we didn't have laws about which side of the road we should drive on or how fast we should go—it would be chaos! And there would be a lot of car accidents where people got injured.

Now imagine that you and your family are late for church. Your dad parks the car, and you're all rushing toward the front door when you spot a small child by themselves, crying. Maybe they got lost, or maybe their parent went inside and doesn't yet realize they're missing. What should you do? Do you think God would want you to comfort the child even if it meant you'd be missing the first part of church service? (Have kids share.)

When we give the law too much power, we can leave people behind. God wants us all to stay together and cross over the finish line with as many believers as possible. In heaven, the more the merrier!

Prayer

God, let me lead with love in all I do. It isn't up to me to tell others that they are right or wrong, though I want to sometimes. Instead of looking for other people's faults, let me do what you did and focus on comforting those in pain, listening to those who are lonely, and walking beside those who have no one with them. Amen.

Bible Verse

I have fought the good fight, I have finished the race, and I have remained faithful.
2 TIMOTHY 4:7

Good Pharisees

Look beneath the surface so you can judge correctly.
JOHN 7:24

Many of the Pharisees feel threatened by Jesus, but not all of them do. Nicodemus defends Jesus many times against his fellow religious leaders. In the film, a short older Pharisee, who we later learn is Joseph of Arimathea, makes a number of comments to defend what John the Baptist and Jesus are doing.

When one of the leaders angrily points out that even some of the Pharisees have gone to see John the Baptist, Joseph remarks, "Maybe they see something we don't." Later, when Joseph finds out that John was killed, he feels bad, because he thought the Baptizer seemed nice.

When discussing groups of people, we have to be careful not to assume that everyone in the group feels and acts the same way. How would you react if someone said, "Only girls are good at math" or "Girls aren't good at soccer." That's not true, and more than that, it is offensive to boys who are good at math and girls who are good at soccer.

When we talk about people who are different from us, we should be careful not to assume things about them. Instead, we should lead with kindness and give them the benefit of the doubt. Going back to the soccer example, since many girls are good at soccer, we shouldn't make statements that assume they are not and that lump them into a certain category.

Few things make people angrier—or are more unfair—than assuming someone feels one way without asking them personally. People are more complicated than that. We show wisdom when we are careful with our words.

Questions for Discussion

It's easy—and natural—to want to draw broad conclusions about people. But that doesn't make it right. Think of a negative conclusion you've drawn about a group of people and share it with your mom or dad.

Ask them why it's wrong to do this.

Prayer

Jesus, you see each one of us as an individual, and you never judge us based on our gender, our race, the country we live in, or how much money we make. You love all of us and desire to know us even more. Jesus, I want to be curious, not judgmental, when I meet new people who are different from me. You met all kinds of people when you traveled around, and each time, you made an effort to get to know the person individually. I want to do that too. Help me grow in wisdom, Lord. Amen.

Bible Verse

Are we not all children of the same Father? Are we not all created by the same God? Then why do we betray each other, violating the covenant of our ancestors?
MALACHI 2:10

Faith shows the reality of what we hope for; it is the evidence of things we cannot see.
HEBREWS 11:1

John recognizes the man at the fishmonger stall who pointed him to a shortcut. He confronts the man and says, "You sent me down that alley. If I hadn't gone that way, none of this bad stuff would have happened to my family." The man responds by saying, "Sometimes the right path isn't the easy path. Just because something seems broken doesn't mean it can't be fixed."

John doesn't yet know this man is Jesus. When they realize they both know John the Baptizer, John shares his confusion about whether or not he believes the Messiah is real or just a story, like his papa thinks. He comments on how John the Baptist made a choice, a choice to believe.

Discussion

Our feelings influence what we think. For example, if we feel uncertain about how to answer a problem on a math test, we may think we didn't do well on the test. God gave us our feelings to help us make sense of things. But sometimes our feelings can lead us in the wrong direction. If someone we love lets us down, we may feel we can't trust them. However, everyone makes mistakes, and we should give others a second chance. Our feelings aren't always right.

The author of Hebrews tells us faith is having confidence in what we cannot see. When it comes to believing God is real, we can't prove it using scientific experiments. We can't use a ruler, thermometer, petri dish, or camera to document and measure God. Our knowledge of God requires something that can't be touched or seen. It takes a leap of faith.

Ask your parents what the hardest part was for them when they chose to believe Jesus is who he says he is. What made them decide to choose anyway?

Have you made your choice?

Prayer

Jesus, thank you for listening to my prayers. Forgive me for the times when my faith has been weak. I may have questions, but I know you'd rather I talk to you about them instead of hiding them. Send me friends my age who I can talk to about you. And I pray for other kids who may have never heard of you. Please reveal yourself to them.

Bible Verse

Anything is possible if a person believes.
MARK 9:23

Then Jesus was led by the Spirit into the wilderness to be tempted there by the devil. For forty days and forty nights he fasted and became very hungry.
MATTHEW 4:1-2

After Jesus' baptism, but before his first miracle at the wedding at Cana, Jesus goes to the desert to spend time alone for forty days. During this time, he fasts and prays to prepare for the next three years of missionary work.

After the forty days, Jesus is very hungry.

Then, the devil comes to tempt Jesus to turn the stones into bread to eat, but Jesus says no.

Then the devil challenges him by leading him to the top of the temple and telling him to jump off and see if angels will protect his fall. Jesus says no.

Finally, the devil takes Jesus to the top of a mountain and offers him all the kingdoms of the world, but Jesus again tells him no.

With each temptation, Jesus quotes a verse from Scripture that disputes the devil's request.

What can we learn from Jesus' response?

Jesus is 100 percent human and 100 percent God. Though it's tough to wrap our minds around that idea, it's important because when we think about what Jesus goes through, we have to remember he is like us in every way except he does not sin. Like Jesus, we will be tempted by things in this life. But Jesus shows us that we have the strength to resist temptation. We also learn that we can turn to God for help in times of trouble. Reciting Scripture, as Jesus does, grounds us in the truth.

Questions for Discussion

When was the last time you felt tempted? Have you noticed one thing your temptations might revolve around—like maybe eating too many sweets, lying, or playing a video game you know your parents wouldn't want you playing?

Find a Bible verse to memorize and recite so you can rely on God's strength to fight off the temptation.

Prayer

Jesus, I will call on you the next time I feel tempted. I know I can always count on you to steer me in the right direction. Thanks for always being available to me, Lord. Amen.

Bible Verse

And remember, when you are being tempted, do not say, "God is tempting me." God is never tempted to do wrong, and he never tempts anyone else. Temptation comes from our own desires, which entice us and drag us away. These desires give birth to sinful actions. And when sin is allowed to grow, it gives birth to death. So don't be misled, my dear brothers and sisters. Whatever is good and perfect is a gift coming down to us from God our Father, who created all the lights in the heavens.
He never changes or casts a shifting shadow.
JAMES 1:13-17

Save the Best for Last 20

Jesus told the servants, "Fill the jars with water." When the jars had been filled, he said, "Now dip some out, and take it to the master of ceremonies." So the servants followed his instructions. When the master of ceremonies tasted the water that was now wine, not knowing where it had come from (though, of course, the servants knew), he called the bridegroom over. "A host always serves the best wine first," he said. "Then, when everyone has had a lot to drink, he brings out the less expensive wine. But you have kept the best until now!"

JOHN 2:7-10

While at the wedding, the hosts run out of wine. Wine was an important part of a Hebrew wedding as its quality was a reflection on the hosts and the amount of money they spent on the celebration. This was a really big deal. Jesus' mother Mary knows how embarrassed the hosts would feel if the guests found out the wine was gone, so to help protect their reputation, she talks to Jesus. Maybe she has an idea that Jesus can do something about it? Later, Mary tells the servers to do whatever Jesus tells them to do.

Discussion

This is Jesus' first miracle, and we learn something important about God's character in this story. When Jesus turns the water into wine, he doesn't just turn it into the same wine the guests have been drinking all night. He turns it into the most delicious, most expensive wine possible. The master of the feast, who is like an event coordinator, even stops the party and remarks that the hosts have saved the best for last.

Why do you think Jesus decided to perform his first miracle that night? (Reflect and share before continuing.)

Some believe it's hard to say no when your mom asks you to do something, even if you're Jesus, so that's a possibility.

Why would he choose to give them wine that was such high quality? No one would have noticed otherwise, and if they had, they would have expected the same quality of wine or even a lesser quality. (Reflect and share.)

Could it be that God is using his generosity to show us how he feels about us? How he wants to give us the best he has to offer? When you love someone, this comes naturally. God is letting us know he loves us a lot.

Prayer

Thank you, God, for your generosity. When I think of all I have, I feel deeply cared for. Thank you especially for my parents, who love me with their best and who bring me up in a home that knows and loves you.

Bible Verse

O LORD, what a variety of things you have made! In wisdom you have made them all. The earth is full of your creatures. . . . They all depend on you to give them food as they need it. When you supply it, they gather it. You open your hand to feed them, and they are richly satisfied.

PSALM 104:24, 27-28

Don't forget to show hospitality to strangers, for some who have done this have entertained angels without realizing it!
HEBREWS 13:2

When John and Andrew go looking for the Messiah, John doesn't realize he's already met him. Jesus was the stranger fixing the stall for the fishmonger who pointed out the shortcut to John.

Have you ever wondered what it must have been like to be told your whole life that once the Messiah comes, all your people's problems will go away? The Jews would be able to rise up against Rome and force them out. They wouldn't have to pay taxes anymore or be oppressed by a foreign country. They could be free and rule themselves.

Questions for Discussion

Impostors had come before saying they were the Messiah, but they were looking for attention and power. God sent special signs to let the world know that Jesus of Nazareth was the real Messiah. Can you think of any of the signs? (Before reading on, pause and see if your family can come up with at least three signs. Hint: Think of Christmas.)

- Isaiah 7:14 tells us that a virgin will conceive and bear a son and his name will be Immanuel, which means "God with us."
- An angel appeared to the shepherds and told them that the Savior was born and that they would find him in Bethlehem, swaddled in a manger (see Luke 2:8–12).
- In Numbers 24:17, the prophet Balaam spoke of a star rising out of Jacob (another name for Israel) that would announce that the great king had been born.
- The prophet Micah foretold that the Savior would be born in

Bethlehem, from the house of David, and that he would rule over Israel (see Micah 5:2).

Wow, that's a lot of predictions, and that's not even all of them! And most of these signs came before Jesus was even conceived!

Prayer

God, thank you for sending us Jesus, not as a military leader or a king with a crown who rules the people, but as something much better—the one who saves our souls so we can live forever in heaven with you. Amen.

Bible Verse

I see him, but not here and now. I perceive him, but far in the distant future.
NUMBERS 24:17

So we are always confident, even though we know that as long as we live in these bodies we are not at home with the Lord. For we live by believing and not by seeing.
2 CORINTHIANS 5:6-7

Mary tells John about having Jesus in a manger and all the people who came from far away to see him. People had no space for Mary and Joseph, but the animals made room. John remembers his mom telling him this story. "It's true?" he asks. She says, "Shepherds, magi, believers, they all came to worship this little baby who'd been born among the animals because they knew." John asks, "Knew what?" And Mary replies, "That God rarely shows up in the way you think he will."

John seems to be struggling to decide for himself between what he's heard from his mom and what he's heard from his dad about who Jesus really is. It can be confusing to have to figure out what *you* believe when the people you trust disagree.

Questions for Discussion

When Jesus began traveling around, people were skeptical about who he was. They didn't know what to make of this preacher who called himself the Son of God. Putting your faith in someone can feel risky. After all, what if you find out later that they were lying?

Close your eyes and see what your gut tells you. Is there a chance that he is who he says he is? Could he be the one sent to save not just the Jewish people, but the entire world?

Talk to your parents about your feelings.

Prayer

Making big decisions as a kid is hard, Lord. I feel like I need to decide who you are, but that feels scary. What if I make a mistake? Will you reveal the truth to me, so I have no doubts? Amen.

Bible Verse

When Jesus came to the region of Caesarea Philippi, he asked his disciples, "Who do people say that the Son of Man is?"

"Well," they replied, "some say John the Baptist, some say Elijah, and others say Jeremiah or one of the other prophets." Then he asked them, "But who do you say I am?" Simon Peter answered, "You are the Messiah, the Son of the living God."

MATTHEW 16:13-16

But Jesus said, "Let the children come to me. Don't stop them! For the Kingdom of Heaven belongs to those who are like these children."
MATTHEW 19:14

John returns home with Andrew, and they've brought a big surprise with them . . . Jesus! As John tries to convince his papa to let Jesus help, Jesus observes the situation. Peter with a bad arm, a fishing net, and only three little fish, and Roman soldiers waiting at the dock. Jesus leans over and puts his hand in the water, then says, "Cast your nets into the deep water."

John is eager to obey but can't lift the nets. He tells his papa, "It's him! He's the Messiah!" Then James comes to help cast the net overboard while Zebedee shouts, "No!"

Let's pause here. There's a lot to notice in this scene, but let's focus on John. John knows something his father doesn't, which puts him in an interesting situation. It isn't typical that a child knows something a parent doesn't, yet it seems like Jesus is making a point worth paying attention to.

Questions for Discussion

Have you ever been in a situation where you knew something your mom or dad didn't know? How did that make you feel? Ask your parents how that made *them* feel.

Jesus makes it clear in Scripture that children are precious. In fact, he says that in order to enter the Kingdom of Heaven, we must become like little children (see Luke 18:17)! We are all God's children, and he is our Father. That means that even though you are a kid, what you have to say is important.

Prayer

Even though I am just a kid, Jesus, I know you can use me to do great things in this world. I want to help you accomplish your mission so everyone knows how amazing you are and how much you love us. Amen.

Bible Verse

The LORD replied, "Don't say, 'I'm too young,' for you must go wherever I send you and say whatever I tell you.
JEREMIAH 1:7

"Master," Simon replied, "we worked hard all last night and didn't catch a thing. But if you say so, I'll let the nets down again." And this time their nets were so full of fish they began to tear!
Luke 5:5-6

Fishing is John's family's only source of income, so when Zebedee owes tax money, the only thing to do is to spend more time fishing. More fish means more money. The problem is, the fish aren't biting. When John returns from getting Andrew and brings Jesus back with them, Jesus tells the men to throw their nets in the water.

In the film, seagulls immediately begin to circle in the sky. Do you think that is an indication of anything? When the fishermen pull up their nets, they are overflowing with fish, to the point that the nets are breaking! Jesus interrupts their moment of joy and relief when he says, "It's time, my Kingdom is here. Leave your nets to follow me, and I'll make you fishers of people."

Questions for Discussion

Have you ever gone fishing? Fishing requires you to be quiet and still. Good fishermen have a lot of patience. When you went fishing, did you catch anything?

Can you imagine the frustration of fishing all night and catching nothing? The fishermen must feel tired, hungry, and desperate, knowing they won't have money to pay Rome.

What do you imagine they feel when Jesus, who they've never met, says to throw their nets back in the water. I bet they are annoyed, don't you?

Try to describe what they must feel like when they realize something unusual is going on in the nets . . . and then see *all those fish*!

Act out this scene for your family without using words. Let your face and actions communicate the event.

Prayer

You make all things possible, Jesus. How amazing it must have been to watch the fishermen pull up those nets overflowing with fish. What joy! When I hear stories like this one, it shows the power you have over nature. Even the fish listen to you! You are so powerful; I'm so glad you're by my side. Amen.

Bible Verse

"Just ask the animals, and they will teach you. Ask the birds of the sky, and they will tell you. Speak to the earth, and it will instruct you. Let the fish in the sea speak to you. . . . For the life of every living thing is in his hand, and the breath of every human being.

JOB 12:7-8, 10

Direct your children onto the right path, and when they are older, they will not leave it.
PROVERBS 22:6

John wants to leave with Jesus but needs permission. John tells his papa, "He's helping people. I want to be a part of that." But Zebedee doesn't want him to go.

John continues to try to convince him. "This is my chance to show up," he says.

Just then, Zebedee sees a little fish flopping on the deck of the boat. (Do you remember John's nickname?) Zebedee picks up the fish, and instead of putting it back in the bucket, he releases it back into the ocean.

Why do you think Zebedee lets it go free? Are there any similarities between the little fish and what John wants to do?

Questions for Discussion

It's hard for children to understand just how much their parents love them. There aren't enough words in the dictionary to describe how deep a mother and father's love goes. Even more amazing is that God's love for you is a thousand times deeper than your parents' love for you! It can be difficult for a parent to let a child do something that could be dangerous, even if it's for Jesus.

Children, take a moment and tell your parents what it means to you to be so well loved and cared for by them.

Parents, tell your children one specific quality that you especially love about each of them.

Prayer

Family means everything, Jesus, so thank you for giving me a family that is so special. We may not always get along, but no matter what, the love we have for each other is unbreakable because it is based on our faith in you. Amen.

Bible Verse

Love never gives up, never loses faith, is always hopeful, and endures through every circumstance . . . But love will last forever!

1 CORINTHIANS 13:7-8

Then James and John, the sons of Zebedee, came over and spoke to him. "Teacher," they said, "we want you to do us a favor."

"What is your request?" he asked. They replied, "When you sit on your glorious throne, we want to sit in places of honor next to you, one on your right and the other on your left." But Jesus said to them, "You don't know what you are asking! Are you able to drink from the bitter cup of suffering I am about to drink? Are you able to be baptized with the baptism of suffering I must be baptized with?"

"Oh yes," they replied, "we are able!" Then Jesus told them, "You will indeed drink from my bitter cup and be baptized with my baptism of suffering. But I have no right to say who will sit on my right or my left. God has prepared those places for the ones he has chosen."
MARK 10:35-40

Some of the disciples act a little starstruck when they join Jesus' mission. I mean, who doesn't want to be on Team Jesus? Both Peter and Andrew tell him, "Let me be the first to say I'll follow you into the most unimaginable ordeal imaginable!" It's hard to use words to express just how much we feel sometimes! When we join a team, it's natural to want to be the best player and make the coach proud. But in this case, Jesus isn't looking for an MVP. He tells Peter and Andrew, "To change the world, we need both faithful hearts and a strong foundation."

Jesus is letting them know the importance of having different kinds of people who have different gifts to accomplish the work at hand—that is, sharing the good news with the entire world. Some people are better at speaking to large crowds; some are better at speaking alone with a person. Some of us are like a sprinkling rain, and others are more like a hurricane. It takes all kinds of people to spread the message of salvation.

Questions for Discussion

Did you know that God gave you a very special talent that few others have? Maybe you have more than one. These talents aren't like being able to play basketball well or being able to do the most push-ups in class. These talents are spiritual and are given to you by God to build up the church. You may have an amazing talent for telling others about Jesus, or you maybe be great at taking care of guests who come to your house for a visit. Whatever your talent, just remember, one isn't more important than another—this is not a competition. You just do your part to the best of your ability.

As a family, take turns sharing what you think your spiritual talent is. Ask others if they agree or if they see something in you that you may not see in yourself. Sometimes those gifts like to hide, so if you aren't sure, don't worry—you'll figure this out soon enough.

Prayer

Jesus, if I haven't told you lately, thank you for everything you do and for always being with me. Can I ask you a favor? Will you reveal to me what spiritual gifts you've given me? I think I know what they are, but I'd like confirmation from you. Help me be aware of you when I'm using my gifts. Amen.

Bible Verse

In his grace, God has given us different gifts for doing certain things well. So if God has given you the ability to prophesy, speak out with as much faith as God has given you. If your gift is serving others, serve them well. If you are a teacher, teach well. If your gift is to encourage others, be encouraging. If it is giving, give generously. If God has given you leadership ability, take the responsibility seriously. And if you have a gift for showing kindness to others, do it gladly.

ROMANS 12:6-8

Soon afterward Jesus began a tour of the nearby towns and villages, preaching and announcing the Good News about the Kingdom of God. He took his twelve disciples with him, along with some women who had been cured of evil spirits and diseases. Among them were Mary Magdalene, from whom he had cast out seven demons.
LUKE 8:1-2

Mary Magdalene hears voices and is tormented. She collapses near the disciples and Jesus. When Peter tries to warn Jesus about her, he says, "It's okay, Peter, this is why I came." Then Jesus calls her by name. She asks him how he knew her name. "I see you, Mary," he says. Then he places his hand on her head and says, "Be healed."

When Jesus rescues us from a bad situation, our devotion to him becomes very personal. He knows our pain because he saw us when we were suffering. If he saw us, that must mean he was with us. What comfort that brings, for who else besides Jesus would you want beside you during hard times?

Questions for Discussion

We all go through times when we are sad or lonely, or when our feelings are hurt. This is just part of life. While we can't take another person's pain away, we can be with them as they endure it.

Can you think of a time when someone sat with you when you were upset? How did that feel? Over the next week, pay attention to the people around you, and if you spot someone who could use a friend, consider joining them. When we are kind to people, we are being Jesus to them. A man named William Toms once said, "You may be the only Bible some person ever reads."

Prayer

Not everyone is open to hearing a Bible verse, but I can show them who you are in other ways. I can *be* the Bible verse. God, give me the courage to be a friend to those who most need one. Remind me to be kind and forgiving so they are curious about the reason for my goodness. Amen.

Bible Verse

"How do you know about me?" Nathanael asked. Jesus replied, "I could see you under the fig tree before Philip found you."

JOHN 1:48

For even the Son of Man came not to be served but to serve others and to give his life as a ransom for many.
MARK 10:45

Jesus washes the feet of those who come to hear him speak. The idea of washing someone's feet might seem really strange nowadays, but in Jesus' time, it was common for Jewish people to wash their feet before they entered a house. Everyone wore sandals and the roads weren't paved—but made of packed dirt. Animals walked the roads leaving . . . well, all sorts of things behind them. Washing at the door before you entered a house showed your host that you respected their house. Andrew thinks Jesus shouldn't be washing people's feet. "That's servants' work," he says. But Jesus tells him, "Those who serve others will be the greatest."

Questions for Discussion

Jesus teaches that those who are last will be first in heaven; those who are first will be last. It's upside down by the world's standards. Imagine trying to run a race so you come in last!

The truths Jesus teaches don't always make sense when we look at them from our perspective. But from the perspective of heaven, he's letting us know just how important it is to be people who take care of others, especially those who are poor, sick, hungry. When we care for others, we give of ourselves (our time, our energy, our concern, our money), and self-giving is a Jesus kind of love.

Prayer

Jesus, giving other people things that are mine is hard. But you gave us everything, even when we didn't deserve it. I want to be more like you, so help me to see others the way you see them so I can love them the way you love them. Amen.

Bible Verse

Then the King will say to those on his right, "Come, you who are blessed by my Father, inherit the Kingdom prepared for you from the creation of the world. For I was hungry, and you fed me. I was thirsty, and you gave me a drink. I was a stranger, and you invited me into your home. I was naked, and you gave me clothing. I was sick, and you cared for me. I was in prison, and you visited me." Then these righteous ones will reply, "Lord, when did we ever see you hungry and feed you? Or thirsty and give you something to drink? Or a stranger and show you hospitality? Or naked and give you clothing? When did we ever see you sick or in prison and visit you?" And the King will say, "I tell you the truth, when you did it to one of the least of these my brothers and sisters, you were doing it to me!"

MATTHEW 25:34-40

Some men came carrying a paralyzed man on a sleeping mat. They tried to take him inside to Jesus, but they couldn't reach him because of the crowd. So they went up to the roof and took off some tiles. Then they lowered the sick man on his mat down into the crowd, right in front of Jesus.

LUKE 5:18-19

The house where Jesus is healing has become crowded. John gets an idea for how he can make sure this sick old man sees Jesus. What does this say about John? What does it say about the sick old man?

When the man lands in front of Jesus, he says, "My Messiah, I haven't lived a perfect life, but I couldn't miss the chance to meet you."

Jesus notices the man's withered feet, cramped up and misshapen.

Then the man asks Jesus to forgive his sins.

Let's pause here. The man wants to be healed, but he asks for Jesus to forgive his sins. That seems important.

Jesus puts the man's feet in the water and then says, "Friend, your sins are forgiven."

There seems to be a connection between sins being forgiven and our bodies being healed. Jesus says to the man, "So that you know that I have the power to forgive sins, stand and walk." And the man stands and is wobbly at first, but then leaps into Jesus' arms. What joy he must feel being able to walk again!

Questions for Discussion

Do you think there could be a reason why Jesus heals the man's body and forgives his sins at the same time in this story? It seems like illness hurts our bodies and sin hurts our souls. Jesus, the Divine Physician, wants to heal all parts of us!

In preparation for the prayer, spend a few minutes thinking about your sins. You don't have to tell anyone else—this is between you and God. Think of times when you may have been mean to your sister or brother, been disrespectful to your parents, or ignored your grandma or grandpa. Or times when you bent the truth too far and it became a lie. Even white lies are lies, and they put distance between us and Jesus. When you're ready, say the following prayer:

Prayer

Jesus, I want us to be close, so I need to tell you about some things that I did that I'm not proud of. (Aloud or in your mind, go through the sins you've committed.) I don't want to do things I know are wrong, but sometimes I do them before I can think! Please help me be more aware so my behavior reflects the light of your truth. Bringing those sins out into the light will allow you to forgive them so I can start fresh. I want to shine your light to the entire world. Thank you for always forgiving me. Amen.

Bible Verse

Let all that I am praise the LORD; may I never forget the good things he does for me. He forgives all my sins and heals all my diseases.

PSALM 103:2-3

Faith of a Gentile 30

When Jesus returned to Capernaum, a Roman officer came and pleaded with him, "Lord, my young servant lies in bed, paralyzed and in terrible pain." Jesus said, "I will come and heal him." But the officer said, "Lord, I am not worthy to have you come into my home. Just say the word from where you are, and my servant will be healed. I know this because I am under the authority of my superior officers, and I have authority over my soldiers. I only need to say, 'Go,' and they go, or 'Come,' and they come. And if I say to my slaves, 'Do this,' they do it."
MATTHEW 8:5-9

Lucius is a Roman guard who doesn't like the scene before him. People gathering on the streets could cause a riot. John sees Lucius and recognizes him as the Roman soldier who chased him when he went to the fishmonger. John runs off and perches on the top of the building where everyone is gathering.

While Lucius is monitoring the crowds, he sees a sick man being carried toward the home where Jesus is healing. The sight of the sick man stirs his heart, and he decides to leave these Messiah-followers alone. A few minutes later, he watches as the sick man walks out of the house, jubilant about being able to walk.

Lucius captures John and drags him off to find Jesus. When Lucius meets Jesus, he says, "He tells me you are a man with the power to heal," and begins to cry. He explains, "My servant, a man very dear to me, lies dying in my home." Jesus asks if Lucius wants him to go heal him. "No, I believe in your authority," Lucius replies. "Thus, if you say my servant is healed, then he is healed."

Jesus says, "This Roman's faith is greater than anyone's in all of Judea." Then he says, "Let him be healed, just as you believe."

Questions for Discussion

Two things about this healing make it different from all of Jesus' other healings. Can you think of what they may be? (Pause before continuing.)

1. The person asking was a Roman soldier, someone the Jews would call a Gentile, meaning they are not part of the Jewish faith and therefore not one of the chosen people.
2. Jesus didn't have to be present for the man to be healed.

The Jews were the chosen people, meaning God made a covenant with them to carry the message of salvation. Jesus came to bring salvation to all people, not just the Jews. This caused some tension. The disciples wanted to know why Jesus was helping their "enemy."

Do you have any enemies? Share with your family who they are and why you think they're your enemy.

Do you think Jesus came to save even your enemy? If your answer is yes, then that means you'll be in heaven with your enemies! Uh-oh. This may be a good time to rethink leaving them in the enemy zone. Jesus wants us to forgive those who trespass against us. That doesn't mean we have to like everyone, but it does mean that we all make mistakes and that we forgive others because Jesus forgave us. Something amazing happens to YOU when you let go of your negative feelings toward someone else . . . you're set free.

Prayer

God, I wish I could get along with everyone, but sometimes kids are mean, and it is hard to know how to react. I pray you would take away all the meanness inside people. If the meanness won't go away, then I pray for those people to know you because you love everyone and your love heals people.

Bible Verse

For Abraham will certainly become a great and mighty nation, and all the nations of the earth will be blessed through him.

GENESIS 18:18

If a man has a hundred sheep and one of them gets lost, what will he do? Won't he leave the ninety-nine others in the wilderness and go to search for the one that is lost until he finds it?
LUKE 15:4

Many people in the region Jesus grew up in made a living as shepherds. A shepherd's job was to watch over a flock of sheep, to make sure they have access to good food and water, and to keep them safe from wild animals and from thieves. Sometimes, sheep would wander off into dangerous areas or get lost. When this happened, it was the shepherd's job to bring that sheep back. Otherwise they'd lose the money that sheep would have brought in. So, when the Pharisees and other teachers of the law criticize Jesus for eating and talking with sinners, he tells them a story about a shepherd with a hundred sheep who loses one. When the shepherd goes off and finds the lost sheep, he calls his friends and neighbors and says, "Let's celebrate! I found my lost sheep!" Jesus finishes the story by telling the Pharisees and teachers of the law that there will be more celebration in heaven when one sinner is saved than when ninety-nine righteous people don't need to repent.

Questions for Discussion

The Bible says that God chose us to be his children even before we were born. He knows everything that happened in the past, he knows everything everyone is doing and thinking now, and he knows everything that will happen in the future. That means he knows all the bad things we have done, are doing, and will do. Yikes! Still, knowing all this, he decided to forgive us and bring us into his family. Isn't that wonderful?

God loves the lost, and he is constantly bringing more people into his family. He didn't just stay in heaven calling for us to come up and join him. No, he came down to experience all the good and bad of life on earth, and he lived a perfect life as a human being, just so he could save us!

Even though there are billions of people in this world, he cares enough that he would have died *just for you*. And just for your neighbor, your friend, and even your enemy.

Is there anyone in your life that you think is a bad person? Have you ever considered that maybe God wants to save that person and to use you to share about Jesus with them? When you think about that, how does it make you feel? Write down the names of people in your life who need Jesus and pray for them to choose to follow Jesus and be changed by him.

Prayer

God, thank you for choosing to save sinners like us! We pray right now that you will save the people in our lives who need you. Thank you for your kindness and your love. Amen.

Bible Verse

In the same way, there is more joy in heaven over one lost sinner who repents and returns to God than over ninety-nine others who are righteous and haven't strayed away!

LUKE 15:7

Then a despised Samaritan came along, and when he saw the man, he felt compassion for him. Going over to him, the Samaritan soothed his wounds with olive oil and wine and bandaged them. Then he put the man on his own donkey and took him to an inn, where he took care of him. The next day he handed the innkeeper two silver coins, telling him, "Take care of this man. If his bill runs higher than this, I'll pay you the next time I'm here."
LUKE 10:33-35

Jesus tells the story of the good Samaritan. A man was robbed and beaten up, left on the side of the road. When a priest comes walking by, the man is so relieved—finally someone to help him! But the priest doesn't stop. Then a Levite walks by, and he doesn't stop either. This is disturbing because Levites are in charge of religious functions. So now two people who work for God have just left him there, alone and injured. The next person he sees walking is a Samaritan. No way would they stop. The Samaritans and Jews have been enemies for generations. But then the unexpected happens. The Samaritan comes to him and cleans his cuts. That alone would have been so kind, but then the Samaritan puts the man on his donkey and takes him to a nearby inn, where he tells the innkeeper to look after him and even pays for everything!

In the film, Jesus says, "You cannot love God without loving your neighbor."

Then he asks, "So, who is your neighbor?"

Questions for Discussion

How would you answer Jesus' question: "Who is your neighbor?" Maybe you'd say the families who live in the houses on either side of you and the one across the street?

It seems like Jesus has another idea of who our neighbors are. In the parable of the good Samaritan, the ones who are supposed to help don't, and the one who isn't expected to help does. What an upside-down situation! It makes you wonder if our neighbors are really anyone we meet. After all, if God is our Father, then those who believe in him are all brothers and sisters.

Share what you think about this idea.

Prayer

If I got hurt, I would want the first person who saw me to come help me. If I saw someone else hurt, I hope I'd run to help them. The men who didn't stop to help probably had important things to take care of, but Lord, I hope I never think of anything as more important than helping someone in need. Thank you, Jesus, for the kindness of strangers.

Bible Verse

"Teacher, which is the most important commandment in the law of Moses?" Jesus replied, "'You must love the LORD your God with all your heart, all your soul, and all your mind.' This is the first and greatest commandment. A second is equally important: 'Love your neighbor as yourself.' The entire law and all the demands of the prophets are based on these two commandments."

MATTHEW 22:36-40

As Jesus was walking along, he saw a man named Matthew sitting at his tax collector's booth. "Follow me and be my disciple," Jesus said to him. So Matthew got up and followed him.
MATTHEW 9:9

Jesus sees Matthew picking up coins scattered on the ground. He says, "God knows your heart, Matthew. Leave this and follow me." Matthew doesn't just set the coins back down. He takes the ones he's holding and throws them down. An action that says, "I'm done with this old way of doing things."

Matthew's situation is a little complicated. He's working for Rome, the enemy of Israel, to collect taxes from the Jewish people. This makes him pretty unpopular with his people. The disciples probably weren't thrilled when Matthew joined their group. He probably had a lot of explaining to do. But God found him worthy because he knew Matthew's heart. When our actions don't match who we want to be on the inside, we can trust that Jesus knows our hearts.

Questions for Discussion

It makes you wonder why Matthew would take a job like that. Was the pay so good that it was worth being seen as a betrayer to your people? Maybe Matthew had no fishing skills and wasn't good at anything but math. Even still, Matthew was borrowing trouble when he took that job.

Maybe the stress of doing that work and the division it caused put Matthew in a state of mind just perfect for someone like Jesus. In the gospel that Matthew would eventually write, Jesus says, "Come to me, all of you who are weary and carry heavy burdens, and I will give you rest." (Matthew 11:28). Do you think Matthew may have felt weary and burdened by his job?

If you had Matthew's job and, one day, Jesus came up to you and said, "God sees your heart. Put that down and follow me," what would you have done?

Prayer

Some of the things I do make me unpopular with other kids. I can be goofy or say something stupid, and it is embarrassing. But I sense that no matter what I say or do, you would never think of me that way, God. You take me as I am, and you know I'm not perfect. You're my safe place, where I can go and be my real self. Thank you for loving me, quirks and all, because you know what's in my heart. Amen.

Bible Verse

But when the Pharisees saw this, they asked his disciples, "Why does your teacher eat with such scum?" When Jesus heard this, he said, "Healthy people don't need a doctor—sick people do." Then he added, "Now go and learn the meaning of this Scripture: 'I want you to show mercy, not offer sacrifices.' For I have come to call not those who think they are righteous, but those who know they are sinners."

MATTHEW 9:11-13

Sermon on the Mount

One day as he saw the crowds gathering, Jesus went up on the mountainside and sat down. His disciples gathered around him, and he began to teach them.
MATTHEW 5:1-2

We talk a lot about the miracles that Jesus performs in the last three years of his life, whether it's turning water into wine, healing the blind, walking on water, or raising the dead back to life. Yet why does he do these miracles? So that people will trust him and listen to his teaching. He often likes to teach in the form of parables—simple stories used to illustrate a spiritual lesson. However, one of his most famous set of teachings is found in the Sermon on the Mount.

When a large crowd comes to Jesus, he goes up a mountainside and teaches them many things. His teaching are so radical, so different, that people are shocked! Jesus tells them to love their enemies, pray for them, and do good to them. He says that love is the fulfillment of the law. He tells them to give to the needy, to be content with what they have, and to store up treasures not on earth but in heaven. He instructs them to judge themselves before they judge others, but to watch out for people who are fake followers of God.

In short, the Sermon on the Mount shows us what a Christian's life is supposed to look like, and it's very different from anything else we've ever seen or been taught.

Questions for Discussion

Today's discussion is going to be a little bit different. The teachings of Jesus are so good that sometimes you just need to hear them for yourself. Today, read some of the Sermon on the Mount as a family and discuss the things that surprise or intrigue you. It's a long passage, from Matthew 5 to Matthew 7, but it's one of the most beautiful sets of teachings in all of history.

Prayer

Thank you, Jesus, for writing your teachings down so that we can be changed by them thousands of years later. We are so thankful for your wisdom and kindness. Help us to walk in obedience to your teachings. Amen.

Bible Verse

"You are the light of the world—like a city on a hilltop that cannot be hidden. No one lights a lamp and then puts it under a basket. Instead, a lamp is placed on a stand, where it gives light to everyone in the house. In the same way, let your good deeds shine out for all to see, so that everyone will praise your heavenly Father.

MATTHEW 5:14-16

Here are the names of the twelve apostles: first, Simon (also called Peter), then Andrew (Peter's brother), James (son of Zebedee), John (James's brother), Philip, Bartholomew, Thomas, Matthew (the tax collector), James (son of Alphaeus), Thaddaeus, Simon (the zealot), Judas Iscariot (who later betrayed him).
MATTHEW 10:2-4

Judas decides to help Matthew collect some of the fallen coins because, as he says, "It's always good to have another option in case things don't go as planned." The disciples traveling with Jesus don't have an income—they must rely on earning money by doing work or by receiving donations from supporters. That means there will be times when they are short on food and hungry or lacking enough blankets and cold.

In that sense, Judas's comment may not seem like such a bad idea. Except, this isn't a regular traveling party; this is Jesus they're traveling with. And one important lesson Jesus is teaching his followers is to trust God for all their provisions. If they bring all their food with them, not only will it be heavy to carry, but they will have no need to trust God to provide the food. By going with little or no money, they are forced to rely on the kindness of strangers or to work to earn some money.

Judas doesn't like this plan.

Questions for Discussion

Let's talk about money. Having plenty of money can offer security "in case things don't go as planned," as Judas remarks. But Jesus doesn't want his followers to rely on their own security because he knows something the disciples didn't know: We trust God a lot faster when we can't rely on ourselves. And Jesus knows God will provide for his followers.

Money isn't evil. Wanting to have a lot of money so you can indulge in selfish things is where evil comes in. This is Judas's problem. When we have money, we are less inclined to rely on God for things. But self-reliance is never going to lead to a close relationship with God. We need him!

What is your view of money? Do you wish you had a lot of it? For what reason? Do you think a lot of money will make you happy?

Ask your parents if they think it is hard for a person who has a lot of money to put God first in their life. Why or why not?

Prayer

I don't earn much money right now, Lord, because I'm still a kid. But I can see how important money is. I pray that I never make money a false idol over who I know you to be. If I earn a lot of money in my lifetime, please remind me to help those who may not have much money, especially the sick, the poor, and those without homes to live in. I want to help others if I can. Amen.

Bible Verse

For the love of money is the root of all kinds of evil. And some people, craving money, have wandered from the true faith and pierced themselves with many sorrows.

1 TIMOTHY 6:10

After dark one evening, he came to speak with Jesus. "Rabbi," he said, "we all know that God has sent you to teach us. Your miraculous signs are evidence that God is with you."
JOHN 3:2

Though Nicodemus is a member of the Jewish ruling council, he doesn't want to take part in bringing Jesus down. Nicodemus is curious about this Jesus of Nazareth and even sets up a private meeting with him, in the dark of night, so no one can see him.

Though the film only shows this in passing, when Nicodemus and Jesus meet, Jesus tells him that no one can see the Kingdom of God without first being born again in water and Spirit (see John 3:5). In Greek, the language used to write the New Testament, the word for *spirit* is the same as the word for *wind*. Jesus tells Nicodemus that the wind blows where it will—we don't know where it comes from or where it is going (verse 8).

Questions for Discussion

The Trinity is Father, Son, and Holy Spirit. God is three persons with one nature. After Jesus dies and is resurrected, he spends time with his followers. Just before he ascends into heaven, he promises to send the Holy Spirit on the Day of Pentecost.

Have you ever felt the Holy Spirit with you? Have each family member share what that was like.

Did you know you can call on the Holy Spirit anytime you need immediate help? Just say three simple words: Come, Holy Spirit.

Prayer

Come Holy Spirit, be with me throughout my day. Keep me safe, help me be kind, and show me the people who need help so I can pray for them. Amen.

Bible Verse

And the Holy Spirit helps us in our weakness. For example, we don't know what God wants us to pray for. But the Holy Spirit prays for us with groanings that cannot be expressed in words.

ROMANS 8:26

That evening the disciples came to him and said, "This is a remote place, and it's already getting late. Send the crowds away so they can go to the villages and buy food for themselves." But Jesus said, "That isn't necessary—you feed them.
MATTHEW 14:15-16

Because of all the miracles Jesus is doing, he and the disciples need some time alone to rest. So, they take a boat across the Sea of Galilee. However, when they arrive, a huge crowd gathers, and Jesus has compassion on them because he sees that they are confused, like sheep without a shepherd. So, he heals the sick and teaches them for many hours. Eventually, everyone starts to get hungry, and the disciples worry about how they are going to feed so many. They suggest that Jesus send the crowd away to go find some food.

But Jesus has other ideas. He says, "No, you feed them."

This confuses them! They reply, "We only have these five loaves of bread and two fish. But how can that feed so many?"

Jesus takes the food, breaks off pieces, and begins handing it out—and he keeps handing food out until all the people are fed. And there are twelve baskets of extra food left over! The people there know that this man has special power. He healed them, he taught them, and he provided all the food they could possibly need. God provides for us in abundance.

Questions for Discussion

Have you ever faced something that God wanted you to do but that you thought was impossible? What was it? What made it seem impossible? And what did God do to make the impossible possible?

Did you know that over 47 million Americans don't know if they'll have enough money to pay for food this year? That's more than one in every ten people in the country!

God can, and will, provide all we need as we obey him in love. He cares for our needs. He sees our struggles. And if he blesses us, he does it so that we can help others.

It may seem impossible to solve the problem of hunger. However, God can use the family of Jesus to make the impossible possible! There are many nonprofits and churches that work to make sure people in America and around the world are fed. Reach out and see if they need volunteers or donate to them if you want to be a part of God's work in feeding the hungry.

Prayer

God, please provide for all our needs and show us how to use what you have given us to help others. We are so thankful for your kindness. Thank you for seeing the things we struggle with and for your faithful protection. Amen.

Bible Verse

Then he told the people to sit down on the grass. Jesus took the five loaves and two fish, looked up toward heaven, and blessed them. Then, breaking the loaves into pieces, he gave the bread to the disciples, who distributed it to the people. They all ate as much as they wanted, and afterward, the disciples picked up twelve baskets of leftovers. About 5,000 men were fed that day, in addition to all the women and children!

MATTHEW 14:19-21

What sorrow awaits you teachers of religious law and you Pharisees. Hypocrites! For you shut the door of the Kingdom of Heaven in people's faces. You won't go in yourselves, and you don't let others enter either.
MATTHEW 23:13

The Jewish leaders are very uncomfortable with the things Jesus says. They feel their positions are threatened and their beliefs are challenged. Do you know what happens when you try to put a tiger in a corner? The claws come out! Jesus is getting too many followers. High priest Caiaphas is ready for blood.

Yet Nicodemus, who is a member of the Jewish ruling council, doesn't seem so bothered by Jesus. Caiaphas tries to turn Nicodemus against Jesus, saying, "Jesus undermines the very establishment that keeps you in power!"

What's really upsetting the religious leaders? They seem to be terrified of losing their positions of power. Wanting to be the one in charge has caused problems since Adam and Eve.

Questions for Discussion

When you're playing with your friends, do you ever have arguments about what to do? One of you wants to go on the swings, another one wants to play basketball, but you all want to stay together, so how do you decide what activity to do? Is one of you more forceful to get your way? Ask your parents if they have to deal with people who try to use force to get their way and hear how they handle it.

No matter who is in charge in your life—your parents, your coach, your teachers, even the president—there is one authority who is more powerful than all of them . . . God. So if you're ever told to do something that you know is wrong, even if the person who asks is in charge of you, ask God to give you the courage to speak up for what you know is right.

Prayer

Jesus, give me the courage to always look to you as the final authority in my life. Help me to know when to speak up and when to remain silent. Send the Holy Spirit to guide my actions. Amen.

Bible Verse

For the authorities do not strike fear in people who are doing right, but in those who are doing wrong. Would you like to live without fear of the authorities? Do what is right, and they will honor you.

ROMANS 13:3

But at a birthday party for Herod, Herodias's daughter performed a dance that greatly pleased him, so he promised with a vow to give her anything she wanted.
MATTHEW 14:6-7

Did you know that Jesus and John the Baptist were cousins? John's mom, Elizabeth, was a relative of Jesus' mother, Mary. Imagine what their family reunions were like! John was the last prophet before Jesus came. A prophet is someone who warns the people to correct their behavior and foretells the coming of the Messiah so the people are ready.

The Pharisees didn't like John because he preached a message that threatened their power. Also, he called them a "brood of vipers," which is a pile of poisonous snakes.

The ruler of Galilee, King Herod, is also no fan of John's. Herod made choices that broke God's commands, and John rebuked Herod for it. When Herod's niece dances for him on his birthday, he is so impressed by her that he tells her he'll give her anything she wants. After consulting her mother, who is angry at John too, she tells him she'd like John the Baptist's head on a platter.

After John dies, the disciples run to tell Jesus what happened.

Questions for Discussion

At some point, we will all experience the loss of a loved one. Every loss is painful, and it takes time to process your feelings. After Jesus hears about his cousin's death, he needs time alone to grieve. Even though Jesus is God, he is also human, and he feels all the emotions we feel.

Have you ever known anyone who died?

Did you know that God didn't invent death? When he created the world, he planned for us to live with him forever—we were created to be immortal. But because we ate from the tree of the knowledge of good and evil, death entered the world. This is why death feels so shocking and devastating.

Tell your family to close their eyes and then read the following passage:

Imagine heaven. Maybe it's a wide-open field with flowers or a huge, iridescent castle with staircases everywhere. Now imagine the moment when John and Jesus see each other for the first time since being alive on earth. What do they do? Do they run up to each other and hug? Do they laugh?

Even though we lose loved ones in this life, for those who love Jesus, we can trust that one day we'll have a moment like this when we are reunited with them in heaven.

Prayer

Today's prayer is a line from a famous hymn from the 1800s written by Horatio G. Spafford.

"When peace like a river attendeth my way, when sorrows like sea billows roll; whatever my lot, thou hast taught me to say, 'It is well, it is well with my soul.'" Amen.

Bible Verse

As soon as Jesus heard the news, he left in a boat to a remote area to be alone. But the crowds heard where he was headed and followed on foot from many towns.

MATTHEW 14:13

That night the Lord appeared to Solomon in a dream, and God said, "What do you want? Ask, and I will give it to you!" Solomon replied, . . . "Here I am in the midst of your own chosen people, a nation so great and numerous they cannot be counted! Give me an understanding heart so that I can govern your people well and know the difference between right and wrong. For who by himself is able to govern this great people of yours?"

1 KINGS 3: 5-6, 8-9

In the film, Jesus and John are talking on a hilltop about John the Baptist's death. Jesus says, "Did you know that the Baptizer's name was John, like you?"

John says, "I guess maybe I never thought of him like that."

"Like what?" Jesus asks.

"I mean, he's this big voice in the wilderness. It's easy to forget that he's a person like me."

Some people seem larger than life. Maybe they have a booming voice, or maybe they have an impressive talent. Some of the most influential people in history have had a certain quality that makes them capture the attention of a room. People like music icon Elvis, basketball player Michael Jordan, or former President Ronald Reagan. In biblical history, think of King David, Samson, or Moses.

Influence comes with a lot of responsibility. When so many people are watching what you do and listening to what you say, you want to share a message that promotes goodness and fairness. This big responsibility requires wisdom from God.

Questions for Discussion

Who is someone you see as a "big voice"? What quality makes them influential?

It is important to remember that people who have big voices are just regular people. We should be careful not to give too much attention and praise to another person because we risk making them a false idol. As Jesus says, "Only God is truly good" (Mark 10:18).

If God gave you influence over other people, how do you think God would want you to use it?

Prayer

In this world, famous people try to capture my attention—through music, movies, TV, social media, and sports. Give me the wisdom to keep from being too starstruck by people. We are all of equal value in your eyes, God. That takes away the pressure to compete or compare. Thank you for that. Amen.

Bible Verse

The rich and poor have this in common: The LORD made them both.
PROVERBS 22:2

Be on guard. Stand firm in the faith. Be courageous. Be strong.
1 CORINTHIANS 16:13

In the film, the high priest Caiaphas decides to arrest Jesus because he's gaining too many followers. He says, "Soon, thousands from these countryside towns will flock to Jerusalem for the Passover festival. If we don't stop Jesus from passing through those city gates, the people will rise up and crown him king. Rome will lose control." Caiaphas gives the order, "Search the area, arrest Jesus, and bring this to an end."

Nicodemus, who is with him, says, "I won't be a part of this," and walks away. He refuses to be part of something he knows is wrong.

In a nearby alleyway, one of Jesus' disciples hears the order and runs to warn Jesus.

Questions for Discussion

Have you ever been at recess and a group of your friends starts to pick on someone? Or have you ever heard a cruel comment directed toward a shy kid in your class?

There are over eight billion people on this planet, and we are all different. Some of us are tall, some are short, some have blond eyebrows, others have hairy feet. Whatever it is that makes you unique can also be used as an excuse to pick on you.

Did you know that most people who pick on others get picked on themselves? When we are hurt, we sometimes want to hurt someone else. But if we don't stop that urge, then we are no better than the bully who started it.

This is where Jesus can help us. When we use our own strength to fight against a wrongdoing, it can backfire. But you have access to a strength that can move mountains. Do you know what that strength is? The power of God's Spirit. Do you know how you call on that power? Prayer.

Prayer

Jesus, some people can be so mean. I wish we wouldn't treat each other with such cruelty. I can control what I do, so give me your strength and wisdom to react with kindness when I'm treated badly. Also, give me the courage to defend the weak and lonely. Amen.

Bible Verse

Give justice to the poor and the orphan; uphold the rights of the oppressed and the destitute. Rescue the poor and helpless; deliver them from the grasp of evil people.

PSALM 82:3-4

"Yes, come," Jesus said. So Peter went over the side of the boat and walked on the water toward Jesus. But when he saw the strong wind and the waves, he was terrified and began to sink. "Save me, Lord!" he shouted. Jesus immediately reached out and grabbed him. "You have so little faith," Jesus said. "Why did you doubt me?"

MATTHEW 14:29-31

The disciples think they see a ghost walking on the stormy waves as they make their voyage, through rain and thunder, across the Sea of Galilee. Terrified, they hold on for dear life so they aren't swept overboard. Then they hear a voice say, "Don't be afraid," and Peter peers out to see that it is Jesus.

"Come, Peter."

Gathering all his courage, Peter steps out of the boat and onto the surface of the water. Shockingly, he doesn't sink! Then Jesus says, "Trust me," and Peter begins walking toward him. After a few steps, Peter takes in his surroundings and realizes the danger he is in. He decides to turn around and head back to the boat. Only, as he tries to return to safety, his feet begin to sink beneath the water. He's going to drown!

Questions for Discussion

Why do you think Peter starts to sink? After all, Jesus called him out onto the water.

What would be scarier for you: to jump out of a boat during a storm or to step off the roof of a high building?

Jesus calls us to trust him, no matter how scared we might be. He will always keep us safe.

Prayer

If you ever ask me to do something for you, even if it is dangerous, give me the courage to say yes, God. I know I can trust you. Amen.

Bible Verse

This I declare about the Lord: He alone is my refuge, my place of safety; he is my God, and I trust him.
PSALM 91:2

Simon Peter answered, "You are the Messiah, the Son of the living God." Jesus replied, "You are blessed, Simon son of John, because my Father in heaven has revealed this to you. You did not learn this from any human being.
MATTHEW 16:16-17

When Peter wakes up, he's on the deck of the boat, the sun is shining, and Jesus is standing over him. He says to Jesus, "Truly, you are the Son of the living God." Peter then bows down in reverence (reverence means a mix of respect, awe, and love), and then so do the rest of the disciples.

At times it is hard to remember that Jesus, our friend, is also Jesus, our Savior. That distinction is important because while he wants to have a close and personal relationship with us, who he is demands reverence, too. This is why inside some churches, it is quiet, candles are lit, and people have their eyes closed in prayer. At the same time, Jesus wants us to be joyful and to celebrate the good news.

Questions for Discussion

In your church, is worship service a time to be reflective and peaceful, or active and joyful? Or maybe it is a mix of both?

Imagine when you finally get to meet Jesus face-to-face. What will you do when you see him? Will you run into his arms, laughing or crying? Will you fall to your knees in reverence? Will you be so shocked that you only stand and stare? Each of you share how you envision that moment.

Prayer

It's hard for me to even imagine what it will be like to meet you, Jesus. You are my friend, and you are also my God. I give you thanks and praise, now and always. Amen.

Bible Verse

Come, let us worship and bow down. Let us kneel before the LORD our Maker.
PSALM 95:6

44 Kingdom Revealed

He replied, "You are permitted to understand the secret of the Kingdom of God. But I use parables for everything I say to outsiders"
MARK 4:11

The disciples are so excited because Jesus announced that it is time for his Kingdom to be revealed. They believe this means no more paying taxes to Rome. They imagine Jesus will enter Jerusalem on a "mighty steed," carrying a powerful sword while the crowds cheer.

Even John says, "Jesus will be raised up and glorified."

But as it usually is with Jesus, all is not as it seems. Yes, Jesus is a king, and yes, he will be raised up and glorified, but not in the way the disciples think.

As they celebrate, Jesus is on a nearby hilltop, praying for them. "They don't know it yet, but things are about to get so much worse," he says.

Though the story is about to get worse, it ends in glory. As we move into the harder part of Jesus' story, don't forget . . . he rises!

Questions for Discussion

When Jesus called the apostles, the twelve men he chose to help him with his public ministry, many others joined them, including women. None of his followers know the tragic events that are upcoming. They think Rome will just move to the side and give Jesus a throne to rule from. But they're in for a shock.

Do you think the men Jesus called to follow him would still have joined him had they known that he would be put to death?

If Jesus had called *you* to be his apostle, what would you have said?

Prayer

Jesus, it is so hard to see you sad and crying. I wish I could go back in time and comfort you. You show us that when we love someone, there may be times when we have to make painful sacrifices. Still, choosing to follow you is the best decision of my life. I will choose you every day. Amen.

Bible Verse

Imitate God, therefore, in everything you do, because you are his dear children. Live a life filled with love, following the example of Christ. He loved us and offered himself as a sacrifice for us, a pleasing aroma to God.

EPHESIANS 5:1-2

Like in the Beginning

He existed in the beginning with God.
JOHN 1:2

When Jesus is praying for his friends, knowing the hard part is about to begin, he speaks about being glorified with God again in heaven, "like in the beginning." Do you know what he's talking about?

The Gospel of John, written by the same young John depicted in the film, begins with these words:

> **In the beginning the Word already existed. The Word was with God, and the Word was God. He existed in the beginning with God. God created everything through him, and nothing was created except through him. The Word gave life to everything that was created, and his life brought light to everyone. The light shines in the darkness, and the darkness can never extinguish it.**
> **JOHN 1:1-5**

This verse is not easy to understand, but first, notice how it starts the same way Genesis starts: "in the beginning" (Genesis 1:1). Jesus is described as "the Word became human" (John 1:14). If Jesus is the Word, then this verse is telling us that Jesus was with God the Father when the world was made and that all things were made through Jesus. Genesis 1:2 also tells us, "And the Spirit of God was hovering over the surface of the waters." The Spirit of God is the Holy Spirit. So in the beginning, the Trinity—Father, Son, and Spirit—was present for the creation of the world. Amazing!

Questions for Discussion

In the film, Jesus says he'll be back with God when he is glorified, like he was in the beginning. Do you get an image in your mind of what this might look like? Describe it to your family.

When you think about the world being created, what do you imagine each person of the Trinity was doing—what specific roles do you think they had?

Prayer

I liked thinking about what it must have been like when the world was created. When I look at the mountains and trees, even the details of a small flower, I know they are masterpieces you made for us to enjoy. Thank you, God, for the beauty we're surrounded by. Amen.

Bible Verse

You are worthy, O Lord our God, to receive glory and honor and power. For you created all things, and they exist because you created what you pleased.

REVELATION 4:11

46 Transfiguration

Six days later Jesus took Peter and the two brothers, James and John, and led them up a high mountain to be alone. As the men watched, Jesus' appearance was transformed so that his face shone like the sun, and his clothes became as white as light.
MATTHEW 17:1-2

John has the special privilege of going to the top of a mountain with Jesus, Peter, and James and witnessing something happen that has never happened before or since.

Jesus' body transfigures! One moment he seems like himself, and the next, his body looks like it is made of light! Then, before their eyes, Moses and the prophet Elijah appear and begin talking to Jesus. Can you even imagine what it must be like to witness this?

Then a voice from heaven says, "This is my beloved Son, with whom I am well pleased; listen to him." This sounds similar to something else God said, when Jesus was baptized.

The disciples are understandably terrified. It's likely none of them were there at Jesus' baptism, so this is probably the first time any of them have heard God speak from heaven. He says that Jesus is his son and that they should listen to him. If the disciples have any inclination to disobey Jesus, that feeling dies right here. You don't argue with God when he tells you something.

Questions for Discussion

When someone who has authority over us tells us something, we might want to argue. This doesn't make us bad people. Being argumentative comes naturally for certain personality types. The world needs people who can argue for what's right! But what about when someone in authority is telling you to do something that you don't want to do? How do you handle it?

Let's do some role-playing. Split the family into two teams. On one side is team authority (let the kids play on this team); the other side is team arguer (that's you, parents). Now role-play a scene where team authority tells team arguer to do something. We'll do this in two takes. (Parents, the point is to show your kids the proper ways to respond to authority—use one take to demonstrate respectful negotiation and one silent obedience. Talk about the differences between the two and how your child's personality type influences how they respond.)

- Take 1: The arguers try to negotiate their way out of obeying, without success.
- Take 2: The arguers show what it looks like to obey even when they don't agree.

Prayer

Lord, I can't imagine what it must have been like to be Peter, James, or John that day on top of the mountain. Moments like this bring a sense of awe and remind me that what I see and touch and feel in this world is not all there is. One day I'll see you in glory along with Moses and Elijah. I can't wait to meet you all in person! In the meantime, I will continue to believe that the world contains much more than just what we can see. Amen.

Bible Verse

But even as he spoke, a bright cloud overshadowed them, and a voice from the cloud said, "This is my dearly loved Son, who brings me great joy. Listen to him." The disciples were terrified and fell face down on the ground. Then Jesus came over and touched them. "Get up," he said. "Don't be afraid."

MATTHEW 17:5-7

47 Jesus Weeps over Jerusalem

But as he came closer to Jerusalem and saw the city ahead, he began to weep.
LUKE 19:41

When Jesus and John approach Jerusalem, Jesus is riding a donkey. "We have very different definitions of 'mighty steed,'" one of the disciples says.

The disciples think Jesus is about to take the throne, become the new ruler of the Jewish people, kick Rome out, and live happily ever after in the land God gave them. Riding a donkey is not exactly an image of power and might. But there is a reason for this.

Jesus fulfills a prophecy given by the prophet Zechariah that says that the future king will come on a donkey (see Zechariah 9:9). In the Gospel of Matthew, we read, "This took place to fulfill the prophecy that said, "Tell the people of Jerusalem, 'Look, your King is coming to you. He is humble, riding on a donkey—riding on a donkey's colt'" (Matthew 21:4-5).

A donkey is certainly a more humble animal than a powerful and stately horse. Perhaps there is a message being communicated here. We receive another clue that helps us know what's actually going on when we see Jesus, distraught as he enters the city gates.

He knows this is the last week of his life.

Questions for Discussion

There are several times in the film when we see Jesus cry. Some people think crying is a sign of weakness, but they are wrong.

Can you recall the last time you cried? What was the situation? Were you embarrassed?

The next time you feel tears bubbling up, remember that Jesus is our role model and if he cried, then it's more than okay for us to.

Prayer

I can't imagine, Jesus, what it must have been like to know that you only had one more week to live. Worse was knowing that you would suffer and your friends would be targeted. Thank you for showing that strength isn't always about muscles and physical force. It often takes more strength to give the gift of yourself to others. Help me to be more like you, Lord. Amen.

Bible Verse

There is no greater love than to lay down one's life for one's friends.
JOHN 15:13

48 Cloaks and Branches

When he reached the place where the road started down the Mount of Olives, all of his followers began to shout and sing as they walked along, praising God for all the wonderful miracles they had seen. "Blessings on the King who comes in the name of the Lord! Peace in heaven, and glory in highest heaven!"

LUKE 19:37-38

When Jesus enters Jerusalem, the people line the street with cloaks and branches. Laying down your cloak was a sign of submission and traditionally happened when a king arrived. Your cloak kept you warm, so by placing it before the king, you were indicating that you'd give of your own resources in his service. The branches came from palm trees. In Jewish culture, palms symbolized their people's past victories.

Palm Sunday is the Sunday before Easter where we commemorate Jesus' entrance into Jerusalem in the last week of his life. On Palm Sunday, Some churches pass out palm branches after blessing them. Palms represent peace and victory.

Then the following February, families bring their palm branches back and burn them at church. The ashes are used on Ash Wednesday, the first day of Lent, the forty days before Easter Sunday. Church leaders use the ashes to paint the sign of the cross on people's foreheads, reminding them that from dust they came and to dust they will return (see Genesis 3:19).

Questions for Discussion

What are ways you show your submission to Jesus? Some common ways include bowing your head, folding your hands in prayer, putting your arms in the air, or kneeling. Showing reverence is a way of acknowledging Christ's divinity while also using your body in the act of worship.

The next time you pray, would you feel comfortable trying a new way of showing your submission to God?

Prayer

You gave us physical ways to pray and show our reverence to you, God. Thank you for all the ways we can worship and praise you—with our bodies, our hearts, our minds, and our spirits. Amen.

Bible Verse

By the sweat of your brow will you have food to eat until you return to the ground from which you were made. For you were made from dust, and to dust you will return.

GENESIS 3:19

49 The Temple

You may not sacrifice the Passover in just any of the towns that the LORD your God is giving you. You must offer it only at the designated place of worship—the place the LORD your God chooses for his name to be honored. Sacrifice it there in the evening as the sun goes down on the anniversary of your exodus from Egypt.
DEUTERONOMY 16:5-6

The Jewish people made an annual pilgrimage to Jerusalem to celebrate the Passover, the time when God saved the Hebrew people from the angel of death by having them mark their doors with the blood of a lamb (see Exodus 12). During their yearly trip to Jerusalem, families sacrificed an unblemished lamb in exchange for the forgiveness of their sins. The temple was the only place these sacrifices could be made.

When Jesus enters Jerusalem for his final week, thousands of Jews are gathered, which makes the religious leaders all the more eager to arrest Jesus. The more people he preaches to, the more followers he gains. Rome and the Pharisees want to shut him down.

Questions for Discussion

Do you remember when John the Baptist baptizes Jesus and he calls him, "The Lamb of God who takes away the sin of the world" (John 1:29)? Do you think it is strange that John calls Jesus a lamb? Why do you think John says that? Do you think it is related to what Jesus says at the last supper about becoming the sacrifice?

Does it feel strange to compare Jesus to a lamb instead of something fiercer? Does Jesus' true strength come with flexing his muscles? How does Jesus show his true strength?

Given Jesus' view of strength, what are some ways you can be strong that don't include you showing your muscles? What takes more strength—yelling at someone or holding your tongue?

Prayer

You are the Lamb of God, Jesus, who gave yourself up for us so we could be reconciled with the Father and spend eternity in heaven. How can we ever thank you enough? Let us start with this: Thank you for taking the fall for something you didn't do, all out of love for us. This is what true strength looks like. Amen.

Bible Verse

You were dead because of your sins and because your sinful nature was not yet cut away. Then God made you alive with Christ, for he forgave all our sins. He canceled the record of the charges against us and took it away by nailing it to the cross.

COLOSSIANS 2:13-14

50 The New Temple

But the Jewish leaders demanded, "What are you doing? If God gave you authority to do this, show us a miraculous sign to prove it." "All right," Jesus replied. "Destroy this temple, and in three days I will raise it up." "What!" they exclaimed. "It has taken forty-six years to build this Temple, and you can rebuild it in three days?" But when Jesus said "this temple," he meant his own body.

JOHN 2:18-21

For the Jews, the Temple was considered the most holy place on earth because they believed it was the only physical space where they could encounter God. The Temple housed the Tabernacle, which held the Ark of the Covenant in an innermost chamber called the Holy of Holies.

In the Gospels, there is one clear moment when Jesus gets angry. He is in the Temple and sees vendors selling animals for the Jewish people to purchase for their sacrifices. When Jesus sees the holy space used for making money and taking advantage of the poor, he becomes righteously angry and drives all the vendors out of the Temple. He tells them, "Get these things out of here. Stop turning my Father's house into a marketplace!" (John 2:16).

The Jews ask Jesus for a sign to prove he is right to do this, and Jesus responds, "Destroy this temple, and in three days I will raise it up." Now this is shocking for the Jews to hear because it took them forty-six years to construct the Temple in Jerusalem. And Jesus claims he can do it in three days?

But Jesus isn't talking about rebuilding a building; he is talking about his eventual death, when his body will be destroyed, and the resurrection that will occur three days later.

Questions for Discussion

About thirty-five years after Jesus died, the Temple in Jerusalem was destroyed by the Romans. Then there was no temple for the Jews to worship in. But thanks to Jesus' sacrifice on the cross, we don't need the blood of animals to atone for our sins. His blood covers all sin—past, present, and future.

Think about the time when Jesus went back to heaven and sent us the Holy Spirit as our Helper. Since we believe in Jesus, the Holy Spirit lives inside us. Do you know what that makes our bodies? Temples!

The way we treat our bodies is important. We may not feel holy, but since the Spirit of God lives inside us, we are!

Knowing this, discuss as a family how you can show your body more respect and care for it better.

Prayer

Holy Spirit, thank you for dwelling in me. I want to be mindful that I'm not alone because I always have you within me! Help me take care of my body in a way that acknowledges your presence inside me. Amen.

Bible Verse

Don't you realize that your body is the temple of the Holy Spirit, who lives in you and was given to you by God? You do not belong to yourself, for God bought you with a high price. So you must honor God with your body.

1 CORINTHIANS 6:19-20

51 The Bread of Life

Yes, I am the bread of life! Your ancestors ate manna in the wilderness, but they all died. Anyone who eats the bread from heaven, however, will never die. I am the living bread that came down from heaven. Anyone who eats this bread will live forever; and this bread, which I will offer so the world may live, is my flesh.

JOHN 6:48-51

The law of Moses required that the Jewish people make animal sacrifices to atone for the offenses they committed against God. Since sin separates a person from God, the chosen people needed to make regular sacrifices to restore their relationship with God.

But the blood of an animal could only be a temporary payment for their sins.

Jesus gathers his disciples and explains that the manna God provided their ancestors in the desert only satisfied their hunger (see Exodus 16). He, Jesus, is the living bread sent from heaven. Anyone who eats his bread will live forever. He explains, "I am the living bread that came down from heaven. Anyone who eats this bread will live forever; and this bread, which I will offer so the world may live, is my flesh" (John 6:51).

When his followers hear this, many of them do not understand, so they choose to no longer follow Jesus. Then Jesus turns to his twelve apostles and asks, "Are you also going to leave?" (verse 67).

Peter responds, "Lord, to whom would we go? You have the words that give eternal life. We believe, and we know you are the Holy One of God" (verse 68-69).

Jesus then explains that he will be the ultimate sacrifice that atones for the sins of everyone in the world—past, present, and future. This final payment will reconcile the world to God, covering the sin introduced by Adam and Eve.

Questions for Discussion

Sometimes Jesus calls us to do something that doesn't make sense from a human perspective. In these moments, he's asking us to trust him.

Let's play a trust game called "minefield." Place obstacles like cups or shoeboxes around your yard. Then blindfold one family member and help them navigate the course using only verbal instructions. If they touch one of the obstacles, then the game starts over.

Prayer

Lord, I trust you because I see your character displayed throughout Scripture. You loved us enough to die for us. You fight for us against our enemies. You never leave us to face life alone. Thank you for your goodness. Amen.

Bible Verse

Trust in the LORD with all your heart; do not depend on your own understanding. Seek his will in all you do, and he will show you which path to take.

PROVERBS 3:5-6

John the Beloved

The disciple Jesus loved was sitting next to Jesus at the table.
JOHN 13:23

At the last supper, the Passover meal that Jesus and his disciples shared the night before he died, Scripture tells us that the disciple Jesus dearly loved sat to his right. It is believed that this disciple is John, because he's referred to as "the disciple Jesus loved" throughout the Gospel he wrote (John 21:7). At some point during the meal, John placed his head on Jesus' chest. Jesus loved all his disciples, and any one of them could have gone and leaned their head on him for comfort or to show love, but what we have recorded is that John did it.

In the film, we see John's desire to know more about Jesus, and we watch him remain loyal to Jesus, even when it is dangerous to associate with him. When Jesus is dying on the cross, John is the only one of the twelve apostles who stays with Jesus as he dies. Jesus even trusts John to care for his mother, Mary, which assumes Mary has no others to care for her. During this period in history, it isn't acceptable for a woman to be independent. Women must rely on their husbands and sons to provide shelter, food, and protection. Jesus must think John is pretty special to give him such an important job.

Questions for Discussion

Have you ever imagined which apostle you would have been most like? Would you be like Peter, a bit impulsive but a natural leader? Would you be like Andrew, who was the first to follow Jesus? Or maybe you would have been like John, the one who, when given the chance, chose to lean against the Lord in a display of total love and trust.

Many artists have painted the scene of John laying is head on Jesus. Some show John's head on Jesus' shoulder, others show John with his head against Jesus' heart. There is one that makes it look like John is sleeping on Jesus. To see that one, ask your parents to look up *The Last Supper*, a fresco painted in the late fifteen century by Domenico Ghirlandaio.

Prayer

John was lucky to be so close to you, Lord. But one day in heaven, I'll be close enough to hug you, and I'm looking forward to that. In the meantime, my prayers are my way of getting close to you. You sent your Holy Spirit to dwell inside me, and there's no way to get closer than that! Thank you for being as close as my heartbeat. I love you. Amen.

Bible Verse

When Jesus saw his mother standing there beside the disciple he loved, he said to her, "Dear woman, here is your son." And he said to this disciple, "Here is your mother." And from then on this disciple took her into his home.

JOHN 19:26-27

53 Alone with God

Then Jesus went with them to the olive grove called Gethsemane, and he said, "Sit here while I go over there to pray."
MATTHEW 26:36

When Jesus goes to the garden at Gethsemane, he tells his disciples he needs to go a distance away to pray. Getting time alone with God is important. Prayer isn't just a one-way conversation where you talk to God. Prayer involves leaving space for God to talk to you! He has things to tell you that you can't hear if you're never quiet.

Jesus knows he is about to be arrested, and in order to have the diligence to complete the task the Father has given him, he needs to take time to pray—a calm before the storm.

Questions for Discussion

Do you have a place in your room or in your yard that is quiet? Where you could sit or kneel and spend time undisturbed by others? Have you ever asked God a question and then sat in silence, waiting for him to respond? God doesn't always respond right away. He may let you know he heard you in special ways—through a breeze that you feel on a day that isn't windy or a song that has the exact words you need to hear. God isn't always loud and showy. He often speaks more like a whisper. If you want to hear him, you should spend time listening.

Prayer

Lord, quiet my surroundings and the thoughts in my head so I can hear your gentle voice. I want to hear what you have to say to me. Amen.

Bible Verse

"Go out and stand before me on the mountain," the Lord told him. And as Elijah stood there, the Lord passed by, and a mighty windstorm hit the mountain. It was such a terrible blast that the rocks were torn loose, but the Lord was not in the wind. After the wind there was an earthquake, but the Lord was not in the earthquake. And after the earthquake there was a fire, but the Lord was not in the fire. And after the fire there was the sound of a gentle whisper.

1 KINGS 19:11-12

King of All Kings

"Now tell us what you think about this: Is it right to pay taxes to Caesar or not?" But Jesus knew their evil motives. "You hypocrites!" he said. "Why are you trying to trap me? Here, show me the coin used for the tax." When they handed him a Roman coin, he asked, "Whose picture and title are stamped on it?" "Caesar's," they replied. "Well, then," he said, "give to Caesar what belongs to Caesar, and give to God what belongs to God."
MATTHEW 22:17-21

The Pharisees try to convince Pontius Pilate that Jesus is a threat to his position. They try to incite fear in Pilate by claiming that Jesus plans to dethrone Caesar.

In the film, the Pharisees say to Pilate, "Sir, he is a threat to Rome! The people declare him King of the Jews. King of all kings . . . above our own emperor, Caesar."

Pilate asks Jesus, "Is it true? Are you King of all kings?"

Jesus replies, "My Kingdom is not of this world."

Jesus doesn't seem interested in destroying Caesar or any other king. He didn't come with political aspirations; he came to change hearts. When they try to trap him by asking if it is right to pay taxes to Caesar, Jesus calls them hypocrites.

Money only has value in this world. In the world to come, the only currency will be love.

Questions for Discussion

Calling someone a hypocrite is a serious accusation. A hypocrite is someone who pretends to be good when they're really not. It's sort of like wearing a mask that hides who you really are.

Certainly, the religious leaders are pretending to be nice to Jesus by saying things like, "Teacher. . . we know how honest you are. You teach the way of God truthfully. You are impartial and don't play favorites" (Matthew 22:16). But they don't really believe what they say. They truly are hypocrites.

Do you remember a time when someone pretended like they would never do something bad, but really did it all the time? Maybe they said not to steal, but then stole. Maybe someone acted like lying was bad and shameful and then lied to you.

Prayer

When I think about all the criticism and unfairness you endured, Jesus, it makes my heart sad. People tried to trap you and trick you when all you wanted to do was save them! If I could go back in time and protect you, I would. Thank you for all you endured for me. Amen.

Bible Verse

What sorrow awaits you teachers of religious law and you Pharisees. Hypocrites! For you are careful to tithe even the tiniest Income from your herb gardens, but you ignore the more important aspects of the law—justice, mercy, and faith. You should tithe, yes, but do not neglect the more important things. Blind guides! You strain your water so you won't accidentally swallow a gnat, but you swallow a camel!

MATTHEW 23:23-24

55 Healing the Blind

And when he comes, he will open the eyes of the blind and unplug the ears of the deaf.
ISAIAH 35:5

Long before Jesus walked on this earth, God promised that one day, a Messiah would come to save us. How in the world would we know who the real Messiah was? Luckily, God gave us a list of some very specific things the Messiah would do, like healing the blind! The verse above was written seven hundred years before Jesus was born!

As Jesus travels from place to place, teaching parables and sharing the good news of God's Kingdom, he heals many people of their blindness. Jesus performs miracles first because he wants to help people, but second because he is fulfilling God's promises about what the Messiah would do. When people see him do impossible things that line up with God's promises about the Messiah, they know they can trust what he says.

While Jesus can heal people of their physical blindness, his words can also heal us of our spiritual blindness. And that's even more important.

Questions for Discussion

We can be blind to many things. To someone who is color blind, yellow and green might look like the same color. Other people are blind to their own behavior. Have you ever met someone who said stuff in rude or thoughtless ways without even realizing it?

Jesus came to heal us of our spiritual blindness. God says that we are all spiritually dead because of sin and that the only hope we have is our faith in Jesus. The same Spirit of God that once raised Jesus from the dead now raises us from the dead and gives us new life!

Imagine how different the world would be if you had never heard the name of Jesus. What specifically do you think would be different? Discuss it as a family.

Experts say that almost half of the world has never heard the good news of Jesus. Hard to believe, right? But that's why it's so important that we share our love of Jesus with other people.

Prayer

Lord, thank you for healing me of spiritual blindness. Thank you for showing me your goodness and for accepting me into your family. Help me to see when it's the right time to share my love of you with others. Amen.

Bible Verse

The blind and the lame came to him in the Temple, and he healed them.

MATTHEW 21:14

He is so rich in kindness and grace that he purchased our freedom with the blood of his Son and forgave our sins.
EPHESIANS 1:7

John and the other disciples are sick of Rome. They thought that the Messiah would set them free from foreign rule, and they were ready for it! So, when John catches up with Jesus in the garden of Gethsemane, he says, "Are you going to defeat the Romans, or not? I thought you came to fix things, to make things right." Jesus says, "I didn't come just to fix a broken world, John. I came to fix your broken relationship with God. The only way to free you from darkness is for someone free from darkness to die in your place. A perfect sacrifice." Who is Jesus referring to? Himself!

Questions for Discussion

Have you ever wondered why Jesus had to die on the cross? After all, Jesus never did anything wrong. Why would a perfect God die for broken people like us?

Our sin separates us from God and leads to death. To eliminate that separation, it was necessary for Jesus, the Lamb of God, to die for our sins. Even Jesus himself prayed that if there was any other way, he wanted to avoid being tortured and killed on the cross. But there wasn't another way. Forgiveness of sins had to come through his death.

What are some ways you can show your gratitude to Jesus for the sacrifice he made?

Prayer

Lord, thank you for paying the price for my darkness! Thank you for forgiving and loving me. Change me, so that I only want to do good. And give me the strength to obey you. Amen.

Bible Verse

But he was pierced for our rebellion, crushed for our sins. He was beaten so we could be whole. He was whipped so we could be healed.

ISAIAH 53:5

But I Don't Want You to Die!

The LORD is a shelter for the oppressed, a refuge in times of trouble. Those who know your name trust in you, for you, O LORD, do not abandon those who search for you.
PSALM 9:9-10

When Jesus finally explains that darkness is going to be defeated by his perfect sacrifice, John says, "But I don't want you to die!" Jesus replies, "John, my death is not the end—it's the beginning. I'm choosing this, and I'm asking you to trust me." He offers his hand, and John considers grabbing it for a moment. But this goes against everything he thought the Messiah was supposed to do. He's frustrated not just because he's going to lose his friend, but also because it goes against what he's believed! He sadly pulls away and leaves Jesus all alone.

Questions for Discussion

Have you ever had a hard time trusting God? Maybe there was something in the Bible that you didn't like. Or maybe something happened to your family, and you wondered why. Share a time when you've struggled with your faith and explain why.

God doesn't explain everything to us. He doesn't show us the meaning behind every little thing. But he does ask us to trust him, to have faith that he is in control, and to choose to believe that he is good. Will we choose to take his hand? Or will we walk away from him when things seem hard?

Now, discuss a time when everything seemed wrong but you chose to trust God, and he took care of you. The Bible says that God is faithful, and when we trust in him, he proves himself every time.

Prayer

God, I know that you made the world. You made me and called me to love and trust you. I can't save myself, but you have graciously saved me. Thank you for letting me become your child and help me to trust you when times get hard. Amen.

Bible Verse

See, God has come to save me. I will trust in him and not be afraid. The Lord God is my strength and my song; he has given me victory.
ISAIAH 12:2

58 Let This Suffering Pass from Me

He was despised and rejected by mankind, a man of suffering, and familiar with pain. Like one from whom people hide their faces he was despised, and we held him in low esteem.
ISAIAH 53:3

Jesus goes to pray in the garden of Gethsemane because he knows he's about to be tortured, mocked, and killed. Can you imagine facing this? He knows that his whole life has been focused on this moment. Still, he asks God if there is any way to avoid it. "Father," he says, "please let this suffering pass from me! But if this suffering can't be taken away, please give me the strength to do it." In the end, it is clear that this suffering can't be avoided. This is the only way to redeem the world. So, because he loves both us and his Father, Jesus obeys and prepares to die.

Questions for Discussion

Have you ever had to do something you *really* didn't want to do? Maybe you had to go to the doctor and get shots, or maybe you had to go to the dentist to get your teeth fixed. Jesus knows how you feel!

God wanted Jesus to face things that were extremely overwhelming, and in the end, Jesus obeyed. He let himself be beaten, mocked, and killed so that we could be set free. Jesus knows how to help us because he also faced hard things and dealt with the same feelings that we have.

As a family, talk about a time when you were overwhelmed but God helped you through. Is there anything going on right now that you need his help with?

Prayer

Lord, help me to be strong enough to do what you want me to do. Give me courage to face hard things with peace in my heart. Thank you for living a perfect life and understanding what it's like to live in this dark world. I know you understand how I feel, and that makes me feel seen and understood. Amen.

Bible Verse

This High Priest of ours understands our weaknesses, for he faced all of the same testings we do, yet he did not sin.

HEBREWS 4:15

59 Falling Asleep on the Job

Then Jesus went with them to the olive grove called Gethsemane, and he said, "Sit here while I go over there to pray."
MATTHEW 26:36

When Jesus goes off alone to pray in the garden of Gethsemane, all he wants is for his friends to stay awake with him. Peter makes sure there are no enemies hiding in the garden, then says, "You can count on us, Jesus!" As always, he's very confident in himself. The only problem is that it's nighttime, and they're tired.

Have you ever been *really* sleepy when you were supposed to stay awake? It's so hard! When Jesus returns from praying, he finds his friends asleep. Jesus wakes them and reminds them to stay awake with him. Then he goes off to pray two more times, and each time, he comes back to find them sleeping again! Finally, he wakes them up as he is about to be arrested. Their enemies have arrived.

Questions for Discussion

Have you ever been late for school because you accidentally slept in? Sleep is good, but falling asleep at the wrong time can be a very bad thing. What do you think would happen if you fell asleep while driving?

A lot of life is like that. Good things done at the wrong time can be bad.

When Jesus is facing the most difficult time in his life, all he wants is for his friends to stay up with him as he prays. Instead, they fall asleep. Rest is a gift from God, but the disciples know it is the wrong time to enjoy it—and they still sleep.

Do you remember any times when you did something good at the wrong time? When would have been a better time to have done it?

Prayer

Lord, give me wisdom to see the right times to do good things. Thank you for all the gifts that you've given to us to enjoy!

Bible Verse

For everything there is a season, a time for every activity under heaven. A time to be born and a time to die. A time to plant and a time to harvest.

ECCLESIASTES 3:1-2

60 You Betray Your Friend?

The traitor, Judas, had given them a prearranged signal: "You will know which one to arrest when I greet him with a kiss." So Judas came straight to Jesus. "Greetings, Rabbi!" he exclaimed and gave him the kiss. Jesus said, "My friend, go ahead and do what you have come for." Then the others grabbed Jesus and arrested him.

MATTHEW 26:48-50

Judas is one of the twelve disciples that Jesus chose to be closest to him. He has watched Jesus perform miracles, seen his power, and lived with him for years. So, when he chooses to betray Jesus to get money from Caiaphas, the other disciples are shocked! Judas comes up to Jesus and kisses him on the cheek so that the soldiers know which person to arrest. Jesus looks him in the eyes and says, "Judas, you betray your friend with a kiss?"

Judas drops his torch and says, "Your . . . friend?"

Even though the disciples didn't know who would betray Jesus, it is clearly something that Judas has been thinking about for some time. The Bible says Judas was in charge of the disciples' money bag, and he often took from it to buy himself things (see John 12:6). Clearly, Judas was selfish and didn't care how much his actions would harm others.

Questions for Discussion

Have you ever been hurt by someone you trusted? What happened, and how did it make you feel? Discuss this as a family.

People are often selfish and may not care about how their actions will affect others. The Bible says that every sin is a betrayal. That means that we have all betrayed God at some point! But God has forgiven us of all our betrayals, and he asks us to forgive others too.

Take some time to ask God to forgive you for the times you've betrayed him. Then take time to pray and forgive the people who have done bad things to you.

Prayer

Lord, forgive us for the times we've disobeyed you. Give us the strength and grace to forgive others. We know that if we don't forgive others, you won't forgive us. So help us to forgive those who've hurt us!

Bible Verse

If you forgive those who sin against you, your heavenly Father will forgive you. But if you refuse to forgive others, your Father will not forgive your sins.

MATTHEW 6:14-15

61 Healing the Enemy

But Jesus said, "No more of this." And he touched the man's ear and healed him.
LUKE 22:51

When people come to hurt Jesus, Peter attacks one of them and cuts off his ear. Peter thinks Jesus will praise him for this, but instead, Jesus stops him. "This was never what I wanted from you," Jesus says. "Those who live by the sword, die by the sword! I could have called on my Father at any time, and he would have wiped out all my enemies."

Then, instead of harming the man, Jesus reaches up and heals his ear.

Peter doesn't understand. Why did Jesus stop him? And why did Jesus heal the man? Weren't they supposed to destroy their enemies? And wasn't it a good thing to protect others from harm?

Questions for Discussion

Have you ever gotten mad when a bully was mean to you? Did you want to yell at them, or maybe even hit them?

If someone pushes us, our natural reaction is to push them back—and harder! But Jesus says that if someone hits us, we should let them hit us *again*. And if they say mean things to us, we should bless them and pray for them. Why would Jesus ask this of us?

Jesus' real goal is to deal with the darkness inside of us—yes, even the darkness inside bullies! We can't change people, but Jesus can. So, we pray for God to change them, and we don't let their darkness rub off on us.

Prayer

Lord, give us the strength and courage to honor and obey you in a world filled with enemies. Help us to be gentle toward those who treat us badly! And help us to be an example of your love so that people would fall in love with you, Jesus!

Bible Verse

Bless those who curse you. Pray for those who hurt you. If someone slaps you on one cheek, offer the other cheek also. If someone demands your coat, offer your shirt also.

LUKE 6:28-29

We Have to Save Him

You intended to harm me, but God intended it all for good. He brought me to this position so I could save the lives of many people.
GENESIS 50:20

Jesus makes it perfectly clear to his disciples that he is choosing to die so that their darkness can be wiped away. But because they don't trust him, they get other ideas in their heads.

When Jesus is betrayed by Judas and taken away by the temple guard, John turns to Peter and says, "Come on, we can still save him!" As they follow Jesus to Caiaphas's home, their goal is to find out how they can stop him from dying.

Because of their lack of faith, they're not just fighting against the evil of Caiaphas, they're fighting against Jesus himself!

Questions for Discussion

Has there ever been a time when God was doing something in your life that you didn't agree with? Did you still trust him? If you didn't, do you look back now and wish you'd had faith in him, instead?

Has anything so bad happened in your life that you thought you wouldn't make it through? Did you sense God there with you? Or did you think, "Where is God? Why is he letting this happen?"

Jesus' death on the cross was the ultimate injustice. It was the worst thing that could possibly happen, but God often brings good out of bad things. It doesn't change that a bad thing happened, but it does show how good God is. Has God ever brought good out of something bad that happened in your life? Discuss this as a family.

Prayer

Lord God, thank you for promising that you will never leave us. Give us strength to trust you during difficult times, and give us eyes to see when you're bringing good out of something bad. Thank you for all the times you've protected us from things we weren't even aware of. Amen!

Bible Verse

And we know that God causes everything to work together for the good of those who love God and are called according to his purpose for them.
ROMANS 8:28

63 Speak Up!

So be strong and courageous! Do not be afraid and do not panic before them. For the LORD your God will personally go ahead of you. He will neither fail you nor abandon you.
DEUTERONOMY 31:6

When Jesus is captured, Peter doesn't know what to do. Will God save Jesus, or let him be killed? With thoughts swirling in his head, Peter stands by the fire to warm himself. A woman points at him and asks if he's one of Jesus' followers. Peter says, "No, you're mistaken." Then a man tells him to speak up and be honest. Peter says, "I'm not who you think I am." But the crowd is sure he's a follower of Jesus. They get angry, and Peter is afraid they may try to arrest him, too! Finally, he yells out, "I swear I don't know that man in there!" After denying Jesus, Peter was ashamed of himself. But Jesus was kind and forgave Peter, because he loved him!

Questions for Discussion

There are many people in this world who do not love Jesus. Some people even hate those who follow Jesus. God said that we shouldn't be surprised by this. Why? Because they hated him first!

Have you ever been afraid to admit that you follow Jesus? Or was there ever a time someone tried to make you feel foolish for loving him? How did you respond in that moment? Do you wish you acted differently?

Since God forgave Peter, do you think he's willing to forgive you, too?

Prayer

Lord, give me courage and strength when people treat me badly. Forgive me for the times I haven't spoken up for you! I lay down my fear of other people and choose to trust that you will protect me.

Bible Verse

The LORD is for me, so I will have no fear. What can mere people do to me?
PSALM 118:6

64 What Is Truth?

The tongue can bring death or life; those who love to talk will reap the consequences.
PROVERBS 18:21

God cares a lot about the words we say and how we say them. Many times, we use our words carelessly. Sometimes, we even use our words for things that are wrong! After arresting Jesus, Caiaphas tries to convince Governor Pontius Pilate to kill him. And how does he do this? With his words! He says Jesus claims to be the King of all kings, above even Rome, which is true. But he also claims that Jesus wants to destroy Rome, which is a lie. Pontius Pilate questions Jesus. But when Jesus says he speaks the truth, Pontius Pilate says, "What is truth?"

Questions for Discussion

Have you ever lied before? Was it to get something you wanted? Or was it because you were afraid or ashamed of something? (Share a time when you lied and how it affected the people around you.)

Caiaphas also tried to use the truth to hurt Jesus. Have you ever used the truth to hurt someone else? Maybe it was to hurt their feelings, or to get something that you wanted.

How about using words carelessly? Have you ever said something without thinking, then realized too late that those words could hurt someone? How do you think God wants us to use our words?

Prayer

Lord, help me to use my words in ways that make you proud of me. I don't want to lie or hurt others with the things I say. Help me to be kind and to control my words in times when I want to use them in wrongful ways.

Bible Verse

Don't use foul or abusive language. Let everything you say be good and helpful, so that your words will be an encouragement to those who hear them.
EPHESIANS 4:29

65 Why Didn't Jesus Defend Himself?

Pilate sent him to Herod Antipas, because Galilee was under Herod's jurisdiction, and Herod happened to be in Jerusalem at the time. Herod was delighted at the opportunity to see Jesus, because he had heard about him and had been hoping for a long time to see him perform a miracle. He asked Jesus question after question, but Jesus refused to answer.
LUKE 23:7-9

In the film, Jesus is kneeling before the crowd that is shouting for him to be crucified. John is crying, pleading for Jesus to tell them all that he really is the king, their Messiah, so that they won't try to kill him.

But Jesus remains quiet.

It is so hard to watch Jesus resign himself to death.

Jesus was sent by the Father to be the sacrificial Lamb. His death saved us. If Jesus defended himself, he would have thrown away all our lives. He wouldn't do that. He loves us too much!

Questions for Discussion

We will never experience anything as terrible as Jesus' death. Having said that, there are times when we must deal with hard things too.

Think of a time when you had to do a big project for school on a subject you didn't care for.

- Why weren't you excited about the project?
- Was it hard for you to get started on it?
- Did you ask for help—from a teacher or parent?
- Once you started and gained some traction, did you begin to like the project more?
- After the project was completed, how did you feel?

Prayer

As a kid, I don't have the freedom to choose what's best for me. I rely on my parents, teachers, and coaches to point me in the right direction and guide me. I don't always try my best when I'm forced to do something I don't like. But as I think about your silence before the crowd, I see that at some point, you accepted the situation and showed love and compassion to others while enduring pain and heartbreak. The least I can do is try a little harder to do my best, no matter my feelings. Jesus, you're my hero. I want to be more like you. Amen.

Bible Verse

For I can do everything through Christ, who gives me strength.
PHILIPPIANS 4:13

66 Don't Follow the Crowd

Don't be fooled by those who say such things, for "bad company corrupts good character."
1 CORINTHIANS 15:33

It's upsetting to see how quickly the crowd turns against Jesus when he stands before Pilate. Because Jesus doesn't meet the religious leaders' expectations for a Messiah (they thought he would be a regal king full of power and might), they stir up the crowd against Jesus who, to them, appeared weak.

It seems like everyone in the crowd listens to the voices of the ones who want to crucify Jesus.

Except John. It takes great strength to stand up against hundreds and thousands of voices like he does.

God will give us that same strength to do the right thing when everyone is telling us not to. Following a crowd is easy. Following Jesus is harder.

Questions for Discussion

Why do you think the crowd turns against Jesus? Does it make you mad that the religious leaders don't like Jesus?

Have you had an experience where a group of friends wanted you to follow their lead, but you knew it was wrong? What did you do? Or what do you wish you had done? How did you feel afterward?

Divide your family in half. Group one is the "Pizza is amazing" group, and the other is the "Pizza is gross" group. Try to persuade each other that your group's opinion is the correct one. What kind of arguments did you make for pizza? Against pizza? How did it feel to argue back and forth? Who was better at winning the argument? Why? How does this show us the power of the crowd?

Prayer

Jesus, I want to follow you, but sometimes I am influenced by the crowd around me. Help me be brave to do what you want me to do. Amen.

Bible Verse

You must not follow the crowd in doing wrong.
EXODUS 23:2

Set One Prisoner Free

Pilate argued with them, because he wanted to release Jesus. But they kept shouting, "Crucify him! Crucify him!" For the third time he demanded, "Why? What crime has he committed? I have found no reason to sentence him to death. So I will have him flogged, and then I will release him." But the mob shouted louder and louder, demanding that Jesus be crucified, and their voices prevailed. So Pilate sentenced Jesus to die as they demanded. As they had requested, he released Barabbas, the man in prison for insurrection and murder. But he turned Jesus over to them to do as they wished.

LUKE 23:20-25

It is a Passover custom to have Governor Pilate release one prisoner from his sentence. Pilate finds no fault in Jesus, but the crowds are relentless, demanding that Jesus die. Pilate finally lets the crowd decide who to free, and they choose Barabbas, a murderer, instead of Jesus, who is innocent.

What's most interesting about Barabbas is the meaning of his name. *Bar* means "son" and *abba* means "father" in Aramaic, one of the languages spoken in the region at that time. Barabbas's name literally means "son of the father."

Now imagine the irony when the crowd starts shouting that they want to have Barabbas released instead of Jesus. They are pleading for the "son of an earthly father" over the "Son of the heavenly Father." Oh, how the angels must have wept!

Questions for Discussion

In today's world, it can feel like the loudest voices are those against God. At the same time, TV shows depicting Jesus' life, Christian movies, Christian podcasters, Christian music, and Christian social media influencers are gaining popularity.

Never in history has there been an easier way to share a message worldwide. And it can happen instantly. This time, when the crowd shouts in support of the things of this world, let us rise up and send a different message, one that is radical by today's standards, one that we communicate with love and truth: Jesus is Lord.

Prayer

Heavenly Father, let me be an instrument of your message. Give me the courage and wisdom to use the tools at my disposal to preach the gospel in a way that wins souls for you. Amen.

Bible Verse

Loving God means keeping his commandments, and his commandments are not burdensome. For every child of God defeats this evil world, and we achieve this victory through our faith.

1 JOHN 5:3-4

Scourged and Crowned with Thorns

But he was pierced for our rebellion, crushed for our sins. He was beaten so we could be whole. He was whipped so we could be healed.
ISAIAH 53:5

The Old Testament contains many references to Jesus and how he would suffer a terrible death. The prophet Isaiah spoke of a Savior who would be despised and rejected, and "led like a lamb to the slaughter" (Isaiah 53:7). But Isaiah's words also spoke of a promise, explaining that "He was beaten so we could be whole" (53:5).

Jesus' body is badly bruised and bleeding even before he is given his cross to carry. Scripture tells us, "Then Pilate had Jesus flogged with a lead-tipped whip. The soldiers wove a crown of thorns and put it on his head, and they put a purple robe on him. "Hail! King of the Jews!" they mocked, as they slapped him across the face" (John 19:1-3). Both Matthew and Mark use the word "flogged" which means "to whip severely."

The crown of thorns they place on Jesus' head, along with the purple robe, is meant to mock him for being a king. The plant they use to make the crown of thorns is likely the jujube tree, a shrub that grows near Jerusalem. Christian pilgrims who travel to the Holy Land today will often take a branch off this tree and bring it home in remembrance of what Jesus endured.

Questions for Discussion

No one likes to suffer. But suffering is part of life, and if we let it, suffering can bring us closer to God. Who better than Jesus knows what it feels like to be mocked, spit on, hit, and embarrassed? When you feel low because someone has been mean to you, look to Jesus as your role model for how to handle it.

When people hurt him, he did not lash out in anger. He did not retaliate. He showed them kindness when they didn't deserve it. And, in the end, he forgave them.

This behavior is unnatural to us. But with God's strength, we have the power to forgive and choose kindness when others are unkind to us. When we forgive, we see from God's perspective. Pray to see others how God sees them.

Prayer

Jesus, take away my desire to strike back when people hurt me. We are all accountable for our actions, and the person who hurts others will have a lot of explaining to do when they meet you. So, keep my focus there and not on how I can get revenge. Holy Spirit, give me self-control. Thank you. Amen.

Bible Verse

Yet what we suffer now is nothing compared to the glory he will reveal to us later.
ROMANS 8:18

69 Be Compassionate

All must give as they are able, according to the blessings given to them by the LORD your God.
DEUTERONOMY 16:17

Nicodemus is a friend of Jesus who is sad when Jesus carries the cross. He takes his special sash and gently wipes Jesus' face with it because he wants to help. And yet Jesus still struggles under a heavy wooden beam on that long road, while people throw mud at him and holler angry words his way.

Like in the verse above, Nicodemus brings what he already has to show Jesus he cares. In the same way, having compassion means that we help others who are struggling—by giving what we have. God has provided compassion and kindness so we can help others who struggle. Often it doesn't take money to help a hurting friend. Simply being with them, listening to their story, and offering something small—like a cup of water—is how we demonstrate compassion.

Questions for Discussion

Why do you think Nicodemus wipes Jesus' face with his expensive sash? Does his action stop Jesus' crucifixion? Sometimes we help others, and they still face a difficult day. Even so, we are called to help in whatever way we can.

Recall a time when someone gave you something they had (or maybe even just listened to you) when you were sad. What happened? How did that make you feel?

Brainstorm as a family ten different ways you can be compassionate to the people God has placed in your lives. Consider people in your neighborhood, school, local park, church, or sports league. Who is in need? Who is hurting? Who could use a friend? Who might be helped by a meal or money or clothing? Choose one of those people and show them compassion this week.

Prayer

Jesus, thank you for loving me enough to carry the cross. Help me be compassionate this week and open my eyes to the friends around me who are hurting. Amen.

Bible Verse

Pure and genuine religion in the sight of God the Father means caring for orphans and widows in their distress and refusing to let the world corrupt you.

JAMES 1:27

70 Be Sad with Those Who Are Sad

Be happy with those who are happy, and weep with those who weep.
ROMANS 12:15

While Jesus carries the cross toward Golgotha, we see Mary his mother weeping. She cries out, "My boy! My boy!" as Jesus walks past. What a difficult experience for her!

John and Mary Magdalene comfort Jesus' mom. They model the advice in Romans 12:15, to weep with those who weep.

When people are hurting, we may not know what to do. We might feel awkward or scared. To be with someone doesn't mean we do something spectacular. Just sitting with a hurting person helps them feel loved and cared for.

Questions for Discussion

How do you think Jesus' mom feels when she sees Jesus walk by?

Have you ever experienced someone trying to make you smile or laugh when you were really sad? Did it work? Why do you think people try to cheer up those who are hurting?

Choose one family member and have them recall a sad or frustrating day. As they share their experience, take turns sitting with that family member, not saying anything, but simply being there with them. Afterward, ask them if it made them feel better to have someone listen as they shared their hard story. How does that help you know what to do when someone is hurting?

Prayer

Jesus, I don’t like it when people are hurting and sad, but I often don’t know how to love them. Teach me how to sit with a friend in pain. Amen.

Bible Verse

Then Jesus wept.

JOHN 11:35

71 Be with the Broken

We who are strong must be considerate of those who are sensitive about things like this. We must not just please ourselves.
ROMANS 15:1

As the crow caws, John tells Jesus' mom, "He could stop this. He could call on God. He could defeat—"

Mary, Jesus' mom, interrupts, "He's not going to do that, John." She tells him of the prophecies about Jesus, that he would change the world—but with a cost. His death would pierce her like a sword.

She tells John, "I got to be Jesus' mother for his whole life, and now? He needs me to be there with him."

She understands the importance of being with her son as he faces death. To be with someone is to love them, even if it's hard or inconvenient for you.

Questions for Discussion

What do you think John means when he says that Jesus could stop the crucifixion? Jesus chose to continue this painful, scary journey—but he did not do it alone. Mary followed (and so did others) to be with Jesus in his final moments on earth.

Have you ever felt alone when you were hurting? What happened? Be sure to have your parents answer that question, too. Believe it or not, grown-ups have walked through pain, and they know what it's like to feel lonely, too.

Pull out a greeting card, preferably one that's blank inside. As a family, write a note to Jesus, thanking him for dying on the cross for all of you and for being there when you are lonely. Leave the card on your dinner table this week as a reminder of Jesus' love for you all.

Prayer

Jesus, I'm amazed that you died for me. I don't know how to thank you, really. But I am grateful you had friends nearby when you died. Help me to also be there for my friends when they're lonely. Amen.

Bible Verse

Share each other's burdens, and in this way obey the law of Christ.

GALATIANS 6:2

Do Not Abandon the Hurting

If someone has enough money to live well and sees a brother or sister in need but shows no compassion—how can God's love be in that person?
1 JOHN 3:17

John makes the decision to stay with Jesus as he walks toward the place of his crucifixion. Even though he is probably scared, John tells Mary Magdalene, "We can't leave him now." What a powerful decision this is!

Jesus continues his awful journey, despite being beaten and injured—while John follows faithfully behind.

One of the greatest things we can do is to love those who are hurting, to choose to stay with them when they need us the most. To leave them is to abandon them in their time of need.

Questions for Discussion

Why do you think John chooses to still follow Jesus, even though it means witnessing Jesus' pain? How do you think Jesus feels knowing that John, his mom, and Mary Magdalene are following behind him?

Have you ever felt lonely when you were sick or hurting? Remember a time when God sent you a friend or family member to stick by you during your pain. Did having them around make you feel any better?

Imagine a close relative is lonely. Come up with five ways you could show them you love them. What could you do? How would you help?

Prayer

Jesus, there are so many people in the world who are lonely or who need a friend. Open my eyes this week to those I can be with. I want to be a helper and a friend. Amen.

Bible Verse

There are "friends" who destroy each other, but a real friend sticks closer than a brother.
PROVERBS 18:24

Then he said, "Jesus, remember me when you come into your Kingdom." And Jesus replied, "I assure you, today you will be with me in paradise."
LUKE 23:42-43

When Jesus is crucified, two thieves are crucified on either side of him. One of them hurls insults at him, but the other one, as he faces death, cries out, "Silence! We deserve this. That man is innocent." Then he says to Jesus, "Messiah, please remember me when you pass into your Kingdom."

Jesus answers him, "Today, you will be with me in paradise."

The thief on the cross shows us there is always time to cry out to Jesus when we're in need or when we're afraid. He is always available to us.

Questions for Discussion

Sometimes we believe we're so far from Jesus that we can't ask for his help. We think he won't listen to us. But this scene reminds us that Jesus will always listen to us, even when we are thieves! He loves to answer the cries of our hearts.

Ask your parents if they ever had a moment when they felt far from Jesus but they chose to cry out to him. What happened? What did they learn about Jesus when they did that?

Prayer

Jesus, I want to be like the thief who cried out to you for help. Help me remember that even when I feel far away from you or I'm making bad choices, you are always there to listen to me and love me. Amen.

Bible Verse

When I was in deep trouble, I searched for the Lord.
PSALM 77:2

74 Forgive Others

Jesus said, "Father, forgive them, for they don't know what they are doing."
LUKE 23:34

In the movie, just before the Romans nail him to the cross, Jesus says, "Father, forgive them for they know not what they do."

What a powerful thing for Jesus to say when people are insulting, mocking, and trying to kill him. This kind of forgiveness is unusual and outrageously kind. It is hard enough to imagine saying these words to someone who has just tripped you on purpose.

Jesus forgives, even in the darkest moments of his life. He demonstrates what love really is.

Questions for Discussion

Forgiveness means that you are no longer angry at the person who hurt you, that you long for them to be restored to kindness, that you want the best for them even though they are giving you their worst. It is one of the hardest things you can do as a follower of Jesus.

If you are ever unable to forgive someone, that's a good time to call on the strength of Jesus. What is impossible for humans is possible with God. That's what the verse "For when I am weak, then I am strong" is all about (2 Corinthians 12:10). Our weakness gives him room to come into our hearts and do the heavy lifting.

Cut a piece of notebook paper into bookmark-sized strips. Give one to everyone in the family. On yours, write the name of a friend or family member you would like to forgive. Tuck that bookmark into your Bible.

Prayer

Jesus, thank you for forgiving me. Forgiving someone who has been mean to me seems impossible, but with you, I can do anything. With your strength, the next time someone hurts me, let me be able to say the words "I forgive you." Amen.

Bible Verse

Make allowance for each other's faults, and forgive anyone who offends you. Remember, the Lord forgave you, so you must forgive others.

COLOSSIANS 3:13

75 It Is Finished

When Jesus had tasted it, he said, "It is finished!"
Then he bowed his head and gave up his spirit.
JOHN 19:30

As Jesus is dying, the world darkens. The Light of the World says, "It is finished," and everything seems to break apart.

Did you know in Greek (the language the New Testament is written in) the word for "It is finished" is *tetelestai*? It means "to bring to an end" or "to complete." It also means "to pay in full." When Jesus dies on the cross, he completes the work his Father asked of him. He pays the price for our sin—completely.

Before Jesus died on the cross, the gates of heaven were closed because of the sin of Adam and Eve, which we inherited. But Jesus' death forgave the sins of all humankind—past, present, and future—which opened the gates up wide for believers to spend eternity in the Father's house. In heaven, there is no darkness, no pain, and we get 24/7 access to the love of the Trinity—the Father, Son, and Holy Spirit.

Questions for Discussion

How did you feel watching Jesus die on the cross? What do you think he means when he says, "It is finished"? How does his death help you to understand his love for you?

In John 15:13, Jesus tells his disciples, "There is no greater love than to lay down one's life for one's friends." That's what Jesus did for us. He laid his life down for us, even when we were sinful. Romans 5:7–8 says, "Now, most people would not be willing to die for an upright person, though someone might perhaps be willing to die for a person who is especially good. But God showed his great love for us by sending Christ to die for us while we were still sinners." As a family, talk about what it means to be a Jesus follower. Why did Jesus have to die for us? What does his death mean?

Prayer

I am amazed that you call me your friend, Jesus, and that even though I am sinful, you still chose to die for me. Help me understand your death and what it means for me. I pray that every day I remember to be grateful for the gift of your salvation. Amen.

Bible Verse

For the wages of sin is death, but the free gift of God is eternal life through Christ Jesus our Lord.
ROMANS 6:23

Together Matters

For where two or three gather together as my followers, I am there among them.
MATTHEW 18:20

As Jesus breathes his last breath, we see John, Jesus' mother Mary, and Mary Magdalene beneath the cross. They are weeping. They are together. In their pain, they have found each other.

We learn a powerful truth, that whenever people gather with Jesus as their focus, he promises to be with them. That is why it is so important to spend time with other people who love Jesus. When we face difficult days or stressful seasons, having a friend with us helps lessen our worries.

Together is important. Life gets hard when we're lonely or when we feel we have to carry a heavy burden by ourselves. If you feel that way today, try reaching out to someone.

Questions for Discussion

As Jesus hangs his head and dies, how do you feel? How does the earth react to his death?

We (thankfully!) already know the end of this story—Jesus will come back to life. But think about how Mary Magdalene, John, and Jesus' mom must have felt when he breathed his last breath. They didn't know what would happen next. How do you think they felt? What must it have been like to watch that horrible scene, and then see Jesus' lifeless body on the cross?

Does it help to remember that without Jesus' sacrificial death, our sins would have kept us out of heaven? Without Jesus dying, there would be no resurrection! God loved each one of us so much, it was worth it to sacrifice his Son, though it was so painful, so we could all be in heaven together eternally. And Jesus went to his death willingly for us.

Prayer

Jesus, thank you for dying on the cross for me. I can't repay you for what you endured, but with your help, I can try to be more like you. Amen.

Bible Verse

So encourage each other and build each other up, just as you are already doing.
1 THESSALONIANS 5:11

77 Jesus Died for the Whole World

When the Roman officer who stood facing him saw how he had died, he exclaimed, "This man truly was the Son of God!"
MARK 15:39

When a drop of Jesus' blood hits the dusty earth, chaos erupts. The earth shakes. Pillars fall. Darkness envelopes the world. It is as though the earth is protesting the innocent death of Jesus, God's beloved Son. As he is lowered from the cross, his mother Mary embraces him. In response to witnessing all this, the centurion, a Roman guard, says, "Truly this man was the Son of God."

The centurion's words remind us right away that Jesus didn't only die for the Jewish people, but his sacrifice is for the whole world—even the enemies of Israel, the Romans.

This is the beginning of the good news for all of us. The death of Jesus offers salvation for all!

Questions for Discussion

Why do you think the Roman centurion now believes that Jesus is the Son of God?

Is there anyone in your life who doesn't yet know who Jesus is? Remember this scene with the Roman guard and let it remind you that Jesus is for everyone, even those who seem very far away from him.

As a family, write down the names of those people in your circle of friends and family who don't yet follow Jesus. Together, pray that they will meet Jesus and choose to give their lives to him.

Prayer

Jesus, I love that you included all the world when you died. Thank you that I can know you today. I lift up my friend who is far from you and pray you will bring them near. Amen.

Bible Verse

At that moment the curtain in the sanctuary of the Temple was torn in two, from top to bottom. The earth shook, rocks split apart, and tombs opened. The bodies of many godly men and women who had died were raised from the dead.

MATTHEW 27:51-52

Give Gifts to the King

[Joseph] had not agreed with the decision and actions of the other religious leaders. He was from the town of Arimathea in Judea, and he was waiting for the Kingdom of God to come. He went to Pilate and asked for Jesus' body. Then he took the body down from the cross and wrapped it in a long sheet of linen cloth and laid it in a new tomb that had been carved out of rock.

LUKE 23:51-53

Earlier in the film, we see Jesus restore sight to Joseph of Arimathea. Now Joseph offers the family of Jesus a gracious gift—a place to bury him. Joseph says, "My family tomb is the largest in Jerusalem, fit for a king, you could say. I do hope it is, for I offer it now to my king."

When Jesus gives us so much, we can't help but give to others. Matthew 10:8 says, "Give as freely as you have received!" Jesus is a king worthy of our gifts. We see this in the beginning of his story when the magi brought the infant Jesus costly gifts. We see it again when Joseph of Arimathea provides Jesus a resting place.

Questions for Discussion

Why do you think Joseph of Arimathea gives Jesus' family his tomb? What do you think his friends, the religious leaders, think of this big gift? Even though he might get in trouble by siding with Jesus, Joseph gives his tomb willingly. What courage!

Why is it hard sometimes to do the right thing, especially when lots of people want you to do the opposite? Yet God gives us good gifts all the time, and he asks us to do the same. He has given us our very lives and takes such good care of us that we can't help but give to others.

As a family, come up with one person at church who could use a gift of some sort—flowers, cookies, a visit, a repaired car, a bill paid. Work together on meeting that need and, as a family, deliver that gift to them.

If you can't find someone, ask your pastor for help identifying a person or family in need.

Prayer

Jesus, you have given me so much. I want to be generous like Joseph of Arimathea. Help me to know who in my life needs a gift from me this week. Amen.

Bible Verse

They entered the house and saw the child with his mother, Mary, and they bowed down and worshiped him. Then they opened their treasure chests and gave him gifts of gold, frankincense, and myrrh.

MATTHEW 2:11

79 Resurrection

As they stood there puzzled, two men suddenly appeared to them, clothed in dazzling robes. The women were terrified and bowed with their faces to the ground. Then the men asked, "Why are you looking among the dead for someone who is alive? He isn't here! He is risen from the dead! Remember what he told you back in Galilee, that the Son of Man must be betrayed into the hands of sinful men and be crucified, and that he would rise again on the third day.

LUKE 24:4-7

Imagine it is Sunday morning and you wake up early, though it's not like you slept much anyway. The streets are quiet, not many are awake yet, and you walk to the edge of town to Jesus' tomb, carrying myrrh and aloe to prepare his body for burial. Your eyes sting, and your heart is broken.

You enter the tomb only to discover it's empty. Your first thought is that someone stole the body. You feel instant outrage. But before you can say anything, you turn around and see two men with clothes that are glowing. Yes, glowing. They ask you why you would come here looking for Jesus.

Excuse me? you think. *Where else would I have gone?*

This is what Mary Magdalene experiences when she goes to Jesus' empty tomb. Now let's look at what Matthew writes about her experience:

Early on Sunday morning, as the new day was dawning, Mary Magdalene and the other Mary went out to visit the tomb. Suddenly there was a great earthquake! For an angel of the Lord came down from heaven, rolled aside the stone, and sat on it. His face shone like lightning, and his clothing was as white as snow.

MATTHEW 28:1-3

An earthquake? An angel descending from heaven? Rolling back the large stone and then sitting on top of it? Mary rubs her eyes, thinking she is seeing things.

She runs to go tell the disciples, and who does she bump into along the way? Jesus.

Questions for Discussion

Ready to do some role-playing? Take turns as a family playing a different role of this story. One of you be the angel, one of you be Mary, and one of you be Jesus (an easy role since you are not there for most of it). Now stand up and playact the scene. Do a serious version and a silly version.

Prayer

I've wondered why everyone was so shocked that you came back to life after three days, Lord—after all, you told us that would happen. And yet, how unforgettable was that moment for your disciples—to see you raised from the dead! I pray I never lose my sense of awe over these stories in Scripture. Amen.

Bible Verse

Christ suffered for our sins once for all time. He never sinned, but he died for sinners to bring you safely home to God. He suffered physical death, but he was raised to life in the Spirit. So he went and preached to the spirits in prison—those who disobeyed God long ago when God waited patiently while Noah was building his boat. Only eight people were saved from drowning in that terrible flood.

1 PETER 3:18-20

80 Scars

That Sunday evening the disciples were meeting behind locked doors because they were afraid of the Jewish leaders. Suddenly, Jesus was standing there among them! "Peace be with you," he said. As he spoke, he showed them the wounds in his hands and his side. They were filled with joy when they saw the Lord!

JOHN 20:19-20

Jesus has come back to life and is walking around talking to people. The confused disciples gather in the upper room to share their news about what's going on. Guess who shows up.

Jesus!

Did you catch the last phrase in John 20:20? It says, "he showed them the wounds in his hands and side."

His hands and sides showed wounds. Even though he has been brought back to life, Jesus' wounds from the crucifixion remain.

The apostle Thomas isn't there when Jesus visits, but when the others tell him about Jesus showing up, he says, "I won't believe it unless I see the nail wounds in his hands, put my fingers into them, and place my hand into the wound in his side" (verse 25). A week later Jesus comes to the place where all the apostles are, including Thomas. When Jesus sees Thomas, he says, "Put your finger here, and look at my hands. Put your hand into the wound in my side. Don't be faithless any longer. Believe!"

Thomas replies, "My Lord and my God!" (verse 28).

Then Jesus tells him, "You believe because you have seen me. Blessed are those who believe without seeing me" (verse 29).

Questions for Discussion

Do you think Jesus shows his hands and side to prove that it is him? What other reason could he have for keeping his scars? If he can create the whole universe just by speaking, surely he can make his scars go away!

Thomas has to put his finger in the Lord's wounds to believe it is really him. If you could say one thing to Thomas, what would it be?

Prayer

I don't need to see you to believe you are real, God. I believe. Amen.

Bible Verse

The disciples saw Jesus do many other miraculous signs in addition to the ones recorded in this book. But these are written so that you may continue to believe that Jesus is the Messiah, the Son of God, and that by believing in him you will have life by the power of his name.

JOHN 20:30-31

81 Jesus Ascended to the Father

Then Jesus led them to Bethany, and lifting his hands to heaven, he blessed them. While he was blessing them, he left them and was taken up to heaven.
LUKE 24:50-51

Jesus leaves the disciples to ascend into heaven, where he sits at the right hand of God. The disciples watch his ascension in awe, and then they go back to Jerusalem. After such an amazing experience, they want to spend time in the Temple, praising God.

When something astounding happens, a natural reaction is to take time to process it. Before Jesus' ascension, along with assurance that a Helper (the Holy Spirit) will come, Jesus' final words are "And now I will send the Holy Spirit, just as my Father promised. But stay here in the city until the Holy Spirit comes and fills you with power from heaven" (Luke 24:49).

It seems that without the Spirit, the disciples lack the full power they'll need to be effective and safe. To the very end, Jesus concerns himself with our well-being.

Questions for Discussion

Have you ever looked at the sky when the clouds are massive and puffy? As the light streams through the water droplets in the clouds, it casts a variety of colors. They say you can read the clouds to determine the upcoming weather. Imagine looking up and seeing a figure among the light and the clouds. Could it be a trick of the eye, or is that the shape of a man?

One day, everyday people like you and me will glance up and see Jesus descend from heaven, returning to bring us home. When that moment comes, may we all be ready.

Prayer

My Lord and my God, count me worthy to be claimed by you. I don't want to waste my life. Instead, I want to make you proud! Amen.

Bible Verse

Remember what I told you: I am going away, but I will come back to you again. If you really loved me, you would be happy that I am going to the Father, who is greater than I am. I have told you these things before they happen so that when they do happen, you will believe.

JOHN 14:28-29

If you love me, obey my commandments. And I will ask the Father, and he will give you another Advocate, who will never leave you. He is the Holy Spirit, who leads into all truth. The world cannot receive him, because it isn't looking for him and doesn't recognize him. But you know him, because he lives with you now and later will be in you.
JOHN 14:15-17

Right after Jesus ascends to the Father, he sends the Holy Spirit to be with his disciples. Jesus knows we need the extra help. The Holy Spirit living in us gives us the gifts of love, joy, peace, patience, kindness, goodness, faithfulness, gentleness, and self-control.

When we become Christians, we receive the Holy Spirit. In Mark 1:8, John the Baptist says, "I baptize you with water, but he will baptize you with the Holy Spirit!"

The Holy Spirit is the third person of the Trinity. Jesus sent the Spirit to live inside of us forever. The Spirit helps direct us to make good decisions and keep our actions in line with what Jesus modeled. He also works through us to draw others to himself, and to do many other things!

Questions for Discussion

The Trinity is made of three persons with only one nature. It is a mystery—something our human minds cannot fully understand. It helps to think of the three persons as Father, Son, and Spirit, but all the same God.

One way to imagine the Trinity is by thinking about water. Water can be a solid, liquid, or gas, but the chemical compound is always H_2O. So while God has one nature, it is composed of three separate and distinct persons.

When you imagine the Trinity, what image comes to mind? As a family, take ten minutes and sketch any images that come to mind when you think of the Trinity. Share your drawings.

Prayer

I have to admit, the idea of the Trinity is hard to understand. But somehow, I am addressing all three persons—the Father, the Son, and the Holy Spirit—as one when I close my eyes and pray. Father, you are all goodness. Jesus, you are my brother and friend. Holy Spirit, you are always with me, helping me to be a person worthy of being called a child of God. I feel like I am a family member in relationship with you all. Thank you for being my everything. Amen.

Bible Verse

But when the Father sends the Advocate as my representative—that is, the Holy Spirit—he will teach you everything and will remind you of everything I have told you.

JOHN 14:26

83 Jesus' Special Care for Women

There is no longer Jew or Gentile, slave or free, male and female. For you are all one in Christ Jesus.
GALATIANS 3:28

Many of the people Jesus heals or helps are women. Today, that doesn't sound all that unusual, but in the first century, society was patriarchal, meaning that men made the decisions that affected family and society. In general, husbands, brothers, and sons were responsible for mothers, sisters, and daughters. Men weren't allowed to greet women in the street, and many preferred that women stay inside and only venture out to go to synagogue. If a woman earned money, it belonged to her husband.

So, when Jesus speaks to women, it is viewed as highly unusual.

Think of ways Jesus impacts each of the following women's lives:

- the woman with the bleeding problem
- Mary and Martha
- the woman at the well
- Mary Magdalene
- the woman who anointed Jesus' feet with oil
- the woman caught in adultery
- Jesus' mother Mary
- Susanna and Joanna, who support Jesus financially

Fun fact: Women are the first to see the resurrected Christ!

By helping or being helped by, so many women, it seems Jesus is making a point. In God's eyes, we are all of equal importance. As Paul writes in his letter to the Galatians, God has no favorites. Or maybe it's more accurate to say that we are all God's favorites.

Questions for Discussion

Discuss these questions with your family, getting everyone's opinion.

- Do you think the way Jesus treated women impacted his culture at all?
- Do you think men at that time would have been frustrated by Jesus giving women his attention and care?
- At school, at church, or with friends, do you notice girls being treated differently than boys?

Prayer

The way I treat others isn't something I always pay attention to, Lord. Make me aware if I treat any group of people differently so I can stop. Just because the people around me do something doesn't mean that I have to or want to. Give me a mind that is independent, thoughtful, and kind. I ask this in the name of Jesus. Amen.

Bible Verse

Do to others whatever you would like them to do to you. This is the essence of all that is taught in the law and the prophets.

MATTHEW 7:12

84 Spread the Word

Jesus came and told his disciples, "I have been given all authority in heaven and on earth. Therefore, go and make disciples of all the nations, baptizing them in the name of the Father and the Son and the Holy Spirit. Teach these new disciples to obey all the commands I have given you. And be sure of this: I am with you always, even to the end of the age."

MATTHEW 28:18-20

After Jesus comes back to life, he spends time with the disciples and gives them instructions about what to do next. Their directive: Go make disciples of all nations! Teach the world about Jesus and baptize them. This directive is called "the great commission."

Jesus came to save every person, not just the Jews, so a large part of the disciples' missionary work would mean going into foreign lands and speaking with strangers, those who didn't speak the same language, who may not have been welcoming to outsiders.

This was no small task. In fact, it would require a lot of courage because the assignment would put the followers of Jesus in real danger. But they were given two things that would provide them with the help they'd need: Jesus' authority and the Holy Spirit.

The responsibility wasn't just for the disciples two thousand years ago . . . it's for you and me too. If all of Jesus' followers went out and told every person alive about the good news, we still wouldn't be done—because people would die and a whole new population of people who haven't heard of him would be born. This cycle will continue until the end of time.

We must keep sharing and encouraging parents to teach their children, and children to teach their friends, about the Father, the Son, and the Holy Spirit. This is how we usher in God's Kingdom on earth.

Questions for Discussion

Are you familiar with missionary work? If you could become a missionary and head off to any faraway land, where would you most want to go? Would you be willing to learn a new language? If you knew it would put you in danger, would you still choose to go?

Many missionaries today go into areas hostile to the Christian message. Their bravery and trust in God are a shining example to all Christians of what it looks like to obey the great commission.

Prayer

Ask your parents to look up the song "Available" by Elevation Worship. Listen to this song, and if you are comfortable, turn your hands palms up. Think about how available you are to be used by God to spread the good news of Jesus Christ.

Bible Verse

But you will receive power when the Holy Spirit comes upon you. And you will be my witnesses, telling people about me everywhere—in Jerusalem, throughout Judea, in Samaria, and to the ends of the earth.

ACTS 1:8

Our Surprising God

You are the God of great wonders! You demonstrate your awesome power among the nations.
PSALM 77:14

After Jesus is buried in Joseph of Arimathea's tomb, we see John with the disciples, taking up fishing again. They wonder what they should do now that Jesus has died. John says he doesn't quite know, but he recalls what someone once told him: "God rarely shows up in the way we think he will."

John continues, "Jesus won't leave us in the dark . . . his death isn't the end."

We know the cross isn't the end of Jesus. God the Father raises him to life. Imagine how surprised the disciples are to see him living and breathing!

When everything feels hopeless, God brings light out of darkness.

Questions for Discussion

What does John mean when he says, "God rarely shows up in the way we think he will"? How do you think the disciples feel after Jesus' death? What did they expect would happen?

How does Jesus show up in a different way than they expected? (He rose from the dead!) What prayers have you prayed in the past that Jesus answered but in a totally different way than you imagined it? What happened?

On a chalkboard, dry-erase board, or sheet of paper, write out your biggest prayers—the ones that seem impossible for God to answer. Put today's date on each request. Then pray as a family that God would show up in a surprising way as he answers these prayers. Keep this list on the fridge or wherever you'll see it.

Prayer

Jesus, I can't imagine just how surprised the disciples were when they saw you alive! Help me remember that you are able to answer even the most difficult prayers. Amen.

Bible Verse

"You don't have enough faith," Jesus told them. "I tell you the truth, if you had faith even as small as a mustard seed, you could say to this mountain, 'Move from here to there,' and it would move. Nothing would be impossible."

MATTHEW 17:20

This is the message we heard from Jesus and now declare to you: God is light, and there is no darkness in him at all.
1 JOHN 1:5

When John talks with the disciples in the fishing boat, he says, "Jesus won't leave us in the dark." He says Jesus' death isn't the end; it's the beginning. Then we see the stone rolling away from the tomb, light streaming in. Darkness has turned into light!

Sometimes we feel darkness all around us. We have a hard time even imagining that light will come. That's when Jesus does his most powerful work. When we least expect it, he shines light on the dark corners of our fears and helps us to see that life is amazing.

Questions for Discussion

How do the disciples feel while they are fishing? Do you think they are confused? Sad? Brokenhearted? How do John's words turn the conversation around from sadness to hope?

We see the followers of Jesus return to their normal fishing situation, but everything is about to change for them. Their sadness will be turned to surprising joy! This reminds us that "weeping may last through the night, but joy comes with the morning" (Psalm 30:5). Darkness may be temporary, but light always chases away darkness.

Ask your parents to think of a situation that they felt was hopeless but God turned around. What happened? What surprised them? What did they learn?

Prayer

Jesus, thank you that darkness doesn't win. Help me to remember that it cannot last and that tomorrow is a bright new day. I love you because you are light. Amen.

Bible Verse

You are glorious and more majestic than the everlasting mountains.
PSALM 76:4

Jesus told her, "I am the resurrection and the life.
Anyone who believes in me will live, even after dying."
JOHN 11:25

From the shoreline, the resurrected Jesus tells the disciples, "Drop the net over the far side of the boat." These are the same words he shared with the fishermen when he first met them.

John shouts, "It's him! It's him!"

They all come ashore and rejoice, laugh, celebrate, and embrace Jesus.

What surprising joy it must have been to see someone you loved so much, but thought was dead!

That's what Jesus means when he says, "I am the resurrection." He conquered death, was raised to life, and is bringing us life. One day, on "the last day," our bodies too will be resurrected.

Questions for Discussion

Have you ever been to a funeral or a celebration of life for someone you knew? You didn't expect your loved one to come back to life, at least not on this earth. There is a "the end" to everyone's life, including Jesus'. But Jesus surprises his disciples, and all of us, by defeating death and coming alive again.

How do you think the disciples feel when they see Jesus on the beach? How would you feel in their sandals? What a joyful reunion this must be for these friends.

Do an online search of "resurrection cookies," then make them as a family. Talk about how each step in the cookie-making process reminds you of the story of Jesus.

Prayer

Jesus, wow! Thank you for coming back to life! Thank you for reminding me that death doesn't win. Thank you for what you endured so that we may have eternal life. Amen.

Bible Verse

And God will raise us from the dead by his power, just as he raised our Lord from the dead.
1 CORINTHIANS 6:14

Teach these new disciples to obey all the commands I have given you. And be sure of this: I am with you always, even to the end of the age.
MATTHEW 28:20

At the end of the movie, John reminds us of the story of God—that he made light and made us in his image, and that we lived with him in a perfect garden. "But we disobeyed him," he said, "and we chose darkness, and it filled our hearts." This darkness caused us to lose our relationship with God.

"But," he says, "God did not abandon us. He sent us a mighty king—the Messiah. He didn't come to conquer. He came to serve. He didn't come to defeat our enemies. He came to show us how to love them. He didn't come to condemn us in our darkness, but to fill us with his light and lead us back to God. He is the one who defeated death. He is the one who rose again. He is my friend."

What a beautiful friend we have in Jesus. He loves us. He died for us. He rose from the dead. One day we will meet him face-to-face. This is the powerful truth of the gospel!

Questions for Discussion

Why do you think it's important we know the whole story of God (as John describes above)?

God's heart for us has always been to bring us light. The world began with light. Darkness entered in when we chose our own way apart from God. Even in that desperate situation, God chose to send his Son Jesus into the world—as light into a darkened earth. He died, and darkness seemed to win. But it could not overpower the light! Jesus is alive today, and he welcomes us into his family.

At the end of the movie, John prays the salvation poem with his papa. Pray it together as a family. "Jesus, you died upon a cross, and rose again to save the lost. Forgive me now of all my sin. Come be my savior, Lord, and friend. Change my life and make it new. And help me, Lord, to live for you."

Prayer

Jesus, I am grateful for your life, death, and resurrection. Thank you for rescuing me from darkness and welcoming me into your light. I'm so thankful I'm your friend. Amen.

Bible Verse

Do not be afraid or discouraged, for the LORD will personally go ahead of you. He will be with you; he will neither fail you nor abandon you.

DEUTERONOMY 31:8

Ready Your Heart for His Return

Don't let your hearts be troubled. Trust in God, and trust also in me. There is more than enough room in my Father's home. If this were not so, would I have told you that I am going to prepare a place for you? When everything is ready, I will come and get you, so that you will always be with me where I am.

JOHN 14:1-3

At the end of time, Jesus will come back. He will gather up any believers who have died and raise them from the grave. Those who are alive will be taken up with him into heaven. Scripture says he's been preparing our place in heaven.

Jesus tells us not to worry about the day and hour of his return; only the Father knows when it will happen. We'll have our own resurrection, and our bodies and souls will reunite in heaven. No one knows for sure how we'll look in our glorified bodies, but it's fun to imagine ourselves at our most perfect age, when our bodies are in prime condition, free of illness or diseases.

In Paul's letter to the Thessalonians, we read about Jesus' return:

For the Lord himself will come down from heaven with a commanding shout, with the voice of the archangel, and with the trumpet call of God. First, the believers who have died will rise from their graves. Then, together with them, we who are still alive and remain on the earth will be caught up in the clouds to meet the Lord in the air. Then we will be with the Lord forever.

1 THESSALONIANS 4:16-17

Questions for Discussion

Maranatha is an Aramaic word that means "Come, Lord Jesus," and it is often used around Christmastime as we prepare to celebrate the birth of our Savior. Between Jesus' birth and death, we learn a lot about what he did, what he said, and how people responded to him. As we wait in joyful hope for the coming king to take us to his Kingdom, what will people learn about our lives—from what we say, what we do, and how people respond to us? How do you want to be remembered?

Prayer

Thinking about the end of the world makes me a little uncomfortable, and since you don't want us to waste time guessing when it'll happen, the most I can do is get myself ready. As I try to stay ready, Lord, help me to be first to apologize, quick to forgive others, and ready to offer others the benefit of the doubt. Remind me to be respectful and gentle, especially when I'm telling people about you. Thank you for your never-ending love. *Maranatha.* Amen.

Bible Verse

As they strained to see him rising into heaven, two white-robed men suddenly stood among them. "Men of Galilee," they said, "why are you standing here staring into heaven? Jesus has been taken from you into heaven, but someday he will return from heaven in the same way you saw him go!"

ACTS 1:10-11

Instead, you must worship Christ as Lord of your life. And if someone asks about your hope as a believer, always be ready to explain it.
1 PETER 3:15

At the end of the film, John's papa, Zebedee, finally believes Jesus is the Messiah. For some people, it just takes time. Our life is the most valuable thing we own, and giving it over to someone else takes a lot of faith. There are times in Scripture when a person believes instantly and other times when the person just needs to move at their own pace. For example, Philip tells Nathanael about Jesus, but it isn't until Nathanael meets Jesus that he believes (see John 1:46–49).

Nathanael benefits from having a direct encounter with the Lord. Matthew is another example of someone who hears of Jesus but doesn't put his faith in him until Jesus comes up to him and says, "Follow me." And that's all it takes for Matthew to become one of the twelve apostles (see Matthew 9:9).

Questions for Discussion

We can do what Philip did and tell our friends about Jesus. They may already know him but not realize you know him too—now you have something new to talk about! Or maybe you have a friend who doesn't know Jesus, and you can tell them how he's the best friend a person can have. Share the Salvation Poem on the previous page titled "Jesus Is My Friend" to explain who Jesus is.

Identify two or three people who you'd like to talk to about the Lord. A wise person once said to talk to God about your friend before you talk to your friend about God. So pray about it first. See if you feel a nudge from the Holy Spirit about which one to approach and how. A good starting place is to ask them if it'd be okay if you shared what Jesus has done in your life.

The verse from Peter ends with advice that you shouldn't overlook. When we tell others about Jesus, we have to be gentle and show respect. If someone else is of another faith background, you show respect by not putting down what they already believe. There is no room to boast over the fact that Jesus is your Savior because it isn't something we earn. It is a gift we receive through grace.

Prayer

God, I want to tell my friends about you. Please send the Holy Spirit to walk before me and pave the path so my friends are open to hearing about you. I'm glad the pressure isn't on me to say the right words or to be entertaining or compelling. This isn't about me; it's about you. All I have to do is speak your truth and that is enough. You take care of the rest.

Bible Verse

God saved you by his grace when you believed. And you can't take credit for this; it is a gift from God. Salvation is not a reward for the good things we have done, so none of us can boast about it.

EPHESIANS 2:8-9

It's 30 AD and people are expectantly awaiting the Messiah. While Jesus isn't exactly who they imagined, there is something special about him. In beautiful 2-D animation the whole family will love, LIGHT OF THE WORLD retells the greatest story ever told—in a whole new light.